I0003263

Authors
Prof. Harsh Bhor (K.J.S.I.E.I.T SION MUMBAI)
Prof. Uday Rote (K.J.S.I.E.I.T SION MUMBAI)
Prof. Umesh Shinde (K.J.S.I.E.I.T SION MUMBAI)

Operating System

CHAPTER 1
SYSTEM SOFTWARE

Unit Structure

1.0 Objectives

After going through this unit, you will be able to:

- Describe Basic Organization of Computer Systems
- Define Operating system, functions, history and Evolution
- Define assembler, linker, loader, compiler

1.1 Introduction

An operating system act as an intermediary between the user of a computer and computer hardware. The purpose of an operating system is to provide an environment in which a user can execute programs in a convenient and efficient manner.

An operating system is a software that manages the computer hardware. The hardware must provide appropriate mechanisms to ensure the correct operation of the computer system and to prevent user programs from interfering with the proper operation of the system.

1.2 Operating System

1.2.1 Definition of Operating System:

- An Operating system is a program that controls the execution of application programs and acts as an interface between the user of a computer and the computer hardware.

- A more common definition is that the operating system is the one program running at all times on the computer (usually called the kernel), with all else being applications programs.
- An Operating system is concerned with the allocation of resources and services, such as memory, processors, devices and information. The Operating System correspondingly includes programs to manage these resources, such as a traffic controller, a scheduler, memory management module, I/O programs, and a file system.

1.2.2 Functions of Operating System

Operating system performs three functions:

1. **Convenience:** An OS makes a computer more convenient to use.
2. **Efficiency**: An OS allows the computer system resources to be used in an efficient manner.
3. **Ability to Evolve:** An OS should be constructed in such a way as to permit the effective development, testing and introduction of new system functions without at the same time interfering with service.

1.2.3 Operating System as User Interface

- Every general purpose computer consists of the hardware, operating system, system programs, application programs. The hardware consists of memory, CPU, ALU, I/O devices, peripheral device and storage device. System program consists of compilers, loaders, editors, OS etc. The application program consists of business program, database program.
- The fig. 1.1 shows the conceptual view of a computer system

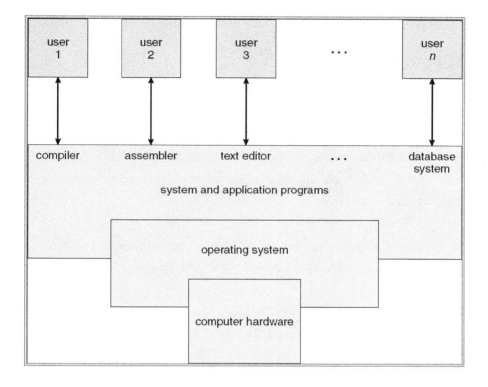

Fig 1.1 Conceptual view of a computer system

- Every computer must have an operating system to run other programs. The operating system and coordinates the use of the hardware among the various system programs and application program for a various users. It simply provides an environment within which other programs can do useful work.
- The operating system is a set of special programs that run on a computer system that allow it to work properly. It performs basic tasks such as recognizing input from the keyboard, keeping track of files and directories

on the disk, sending output to the display screen and controlling a peripheral devices.

- OS is designed to serve two basic purposes :
1. It controls the allocation and use of the computing system's resources among the various user and tasks.
2. It provides an interface between the computer hardware and the programmer that simplifies and makes feasible for coding, creation, debugging of application programs.

- The operating system must support the following tasks. The tasks are :
1. Provides the facilities to create, modification of program and data files using and editor.
2. Access to the compiler for translating the user program from high level language to machine language.
3. Provide a loader program to move the compiled program code to the computer's memory for execution.
4. Provide routines that handle the details of I/O programming.

1.3 I/O System Management

I/O System Management
- The module that keeps track of the status of devices is called the I/O traffic controller. Each I/O device has a device handler that resides in a separate process associated with that device.
- The I/O subsystem consists of

1. A memory management component that includes buffering, caching and spooling.

2. A general device driver interface.

Drivers for specific hardware devices.

1.4 Assembler

Input to an assembler is an assembly language program. Output is an object program plus information that enables the loader to prepare the object program for execution. At one time, the computer programmer had at his disposal a basic machine that interpreted, through hardware, certain fundamental instructions. He would program this computer by writing a series of ones and zeros(machine language), place them into the memory of the machine.

1.5 Compiler

The high level languages – examples are FORTRAN, COBOL, ALGOL and PL/I – are processed by compilers and interpreters. A compilers is a program that accepts a source program in a "high-level language" and produces a corresponding object program. An interpreter is a program that appears to execute a source program as if it was machine language. The same name (FORTRAN, COBOL etc) is often used to designate both a compiler and its associated language.

1.6 Loader

A loader is a routine that loads an object program and prepares it for execution. There are various loading schemes: absolute, relocating and direct-linking. In general, the loader must load, relocate, and link the object program. Loader is a program that places programs into memory and prepares them for execution. In a simple loading scheme, the assembler outputs the machine language translation of a program on a secondary device and a loader is placed in core. The loader places into memory the machine language version of the user's program and transfers control to it. Since the loader program is much smaller than the assembler, thos makes more core available to user's program.

1.7 History of Operating System

- Operating systems have been evolving through the years. Following table shows the history of OS.

Generation	Year	Electronic devices used	Types of OS and devices
First	1945 – 55	Vacuum tubes	Plug boards
Second	1955 – 1965	Transistors	Batch system
Third	1965 – 1980	Integrated Circuit (IC)	Multiprogramming
Fourth	Since 1980	Large scale integration	PC

1.8 Summary

Operating Systems

An Operating system is concerned with the allocation of resources and services, such as memory, processors, devices and information. The Operating System correspondingly includes programs to manage these resources, such as a traffic controller, a scheduler, memory management module, I/O programs, and a file system.

Assembler
Input to an assembler is an assembly language program. Output is an object program plus information that enables the loader to prepare the object program for execution.

Loader
A loader is a routine that loads an object program and prepares it for execution. There are various loading schemes: absolute, relocating and direct-linking. In general, the loader must load, relocate, and link the object program

Compilers
A compilers is a program that accepts a source program " in a high-level language" and produces a corresponding object program.

1.9 Model Question

Q. 1 Define Operating System?
Q. 2 Explain various function of operating system?
Q. 3 Explain I/O system Management?
Q. 4 Define & explain Assembler, Loader, Compiler?

CHAPTER 2
FUNDAMENTAL OF OPERATING SYSTEM

Unit Structure
2.0 Objectives

2.1 Introduction

2.2 Operating System Services

2.0 Objectives

After going through this unit, you will be able to:

- To describe the services an operating system provides to users, processes, and other systems
- Describe operating system services and its components.
- Define multitasking and multiprogramming.
- Describe timesharing, buffering & spooling.

2.1 Introduction

An operating system provides the environment within which programs are executed. Internally, operating systems vary greatly in their makeup, since they are organized along many different lines. The design of a new operating system is a major task. It is important that the goals of the system be well defined before the design begins.

We can view an operating system from several vantage points. One view focuses on the services that the system provides, another, on the interface that it makes available to users and programmers; a third, on its components and their interconnections.

2.2 Operating System Services

- An operating system provides services to programs and to the users of those programs. It provided by one environment for the execution of programs. The services provided by one operating system is difficult than other operating system. Operating system makes the programming task easier.
- The common service provided by the operating system is listed below.
1. Program execution
2. I/O operation
3. File system manipulation
4. Communications
5. Error detection
1. **Program execution**: Operating system loads a program into memory and executes the program. The program must be able to end its execution, either normally or abnormally.
2. **I/O Operation** : I/O means any file or any specific I/O device. Program may require any I/O device while running. So operating system must provide the required I/O.

3. **File system manipulation** : Program needs to read a file or write a file. The operating system gives the permission to the program for operation on file.

4. **Communication** : Data transfer between two processes is required for some time. The both processes are on the one computer or on different computer but connected through computer network. Communication may be implemented by two methods:

   a. Shared memory

   b. Message passing.

5. **Error detection** : error may occur in CPU, in I/O devices or in the memory hardware. The operating system constantly needs to be aware of possible errors. It should take the appropriate action to ensure correct and consistent computing.

- Operating system with multiple users provides following services.

1. Resource Allocation

2. Accounting

3. Protection

A) Resource Allocation :

- If there are more than one user or jobs running at the same time, then resources must be allocated to each of them. Operating system manages different types of resources require special allocation code, i.e. main memory, CPU cycles and file storage.

- There are some resources which require only general request and release code. For allocating CPU, CPU scheduling algorithms are used for better utilization of CPU. CPU scheduling algorithms are used for better utilization of CPU. CPU scheduling routines consider the speed of the CPU, number of available registers and other required factors.

B) Accounting :

- Logs of each user must be kept. It is also necessary to keep record of which user how much and what kinds of computer resources. This log is used for accounting purposes.

- The accounting data may be used for statistics or for the billing. It also used to improve system efficiency.

C) Protection :

- Protection involves ensuring that all access to system resources is controlled. Security starts with each user having to authenticate to the system, usually by means of a password. External I/O devices must be also protected from invalid access attempts.

- In protection, all the access to the resources is controlled. In multiprocess environment, it is possible that, one process to interface with the other, or with the operating system, so protection is required.

2.3 Operating System Components

- Modern operating systems share the goal of supporting the system components. The system components are :

1. Process Management
2. Main Memory Management
3. File Management
4. Secondary Storage Management
5. I/O System Management
6. Networking

7. Protection System

8. Command Interpreter System

2.4 Batch System

- Some computer systems only did one thing at a time. They had a list of the computer system may be dedicated to a single program until its completion, or they may be dynamically reassigned among a collection of active programs in different stages of execution.

- Batch operating system is one where programs and data are collected together in a batch before processing starts. A job is predefined sequence of commands, programs and data that are combined in to a single unit called job.

- Fig. 2.1 shows the memory layout for a simple batch system. Memory management in batch system is very simple. Memory is usually divided into two areas : Operating system and user program area.

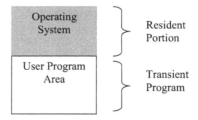

Fig 2.1 Memory Layout for a Simple Batch System

- Scheduling is also simple in batch system. Jobs are processed in the order of submission i.e first come first served fashion.
- When job completed execution, its memory is releases and the output for the job gets copied into an output **spool** for later printing.
- Batch system often provides simple forms of file management. Access to file is serial. Batch systems do not require any time critical device management.
- Batch systems are inconvenient for users because users can not interact with their jobs to fix problems. There may also be long turn around times.

  Example of this system id generating monthly bank statement.

Advantages o Batch System

- Move much of the work of the operator to the computer.
- Increased performance since it was possible for job to start as soon as the previous job finished.

Disadvantages of Batch System

- Turn around time can be large from user standpoint.
- Difficult to debug program.
- A job could enter an infinite loop.
- A job could corrupt the monitor, thus affecting pending jobs.
- Due to lack of protection scheme, one batch job can affect pending jobs.

2.5 Time Sharing Systems

- Multi-programmed batched systems provide an environment where the various system resources (for example, CPU, memory, peripheral devices) are utilized effectively.
- Time sharing, or multitasking, is a logical extension of multiprogramming. Multiple jobs are executed by the CPU switching between them, but the

switches occur so frequently that the users may interact with each program while it is running.

- An interactive, or hands-on, computer system provides on-line communication between the user and the system. The user gives instructions to the operating system or to a program directly, and receives an immediate response. Usually, a keyboard is used to provide input, and a display screen (such as a cathode-ray tube (CRT) or monitor) is used to provide output.

- If users are to be able to access both data and code conveniently, an on-line file system must be available. A file is a collection of related information defined by its creator. Batch systems are appropriate for executing large jobs that need little interaction.

- Time-sharing systems were developed to provide interactive use of a computer system at a reasonable cost. A time-shared operating system uses CPU scheduling and multiprogramming to provide each user with a small portion of a time-shared computer. Each user has at least one separate program in memory. A program that is loaded into memory and is executing is commonly referred to as a process. When a process executes, it typically executes for only a short time before it either finishes or needs to perform I/O. I/O may be interactive; that is, output is to a display for the user and input is from a user keyboard. Since interactive I/O typically runs at people speeds, it may take a long time to completed.

- A time-shared operating system allows the many users to share the computer simultaneously. Since each action or command in a time-shared system tends to be short, only a little CPU time is needed for each user. As the system switches rapidly from one user to the next, each user is given the impression that she has her own computer, whereas actually one computer is being shared among many users.

- Time-sharing operating systems are even more complex than are multi-programmed operating systems. As in multiprogramming, several jobs must be kept simultaneously in memory, which requires some form of memory management and protection.

2.6 Multiprogramming

- When two or more programs are in memory at the same time, sharing the processor is referred to the multiprogramming operating system. Multiprogramming assumes a single processor that is being shared. It increases CPU utilization by organizing jobs so that the CPU always has one to execute.
- Fig. 2.2 shows the memory layout for a multiprogramming system.

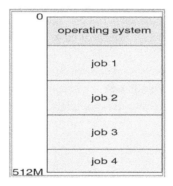

- The operating system keeps several jobs in memory at a time. This set of jobs is a subset of the jobs kept in the job pool. The operating system picks and begins to execute one of the job in the memory.
- Multiprogrammed system provide an environment in which the various system resources are utilized effectively, but they do not provide for user interaction with the computer system.
- Jobs entering into the system are kept into the memory. Operating system picks the job and begins to execute one of the job in the memory. Having

several programs in memory at the same time requires some form of memory management.

- Multiprogramming operating system monitors the state of all active programs and system resources. This ensures that the CPU is never idle unless there are no jobs.

Advantages
1. High CPU utilization.
2. It appears that many programs are allotted CPU almost simultaneously.

Disadvantages
1. CPU scheduling is requires.
2. To accommodate many jobs in memory, memory management is required.

2.7 Spooling

- Acronym for simultaneous peripheral operations on line. Spooling refers to putting jobs in a buffer, a special area in memory or on a disk where a device can access them when it is ready.
- Spooling is useful because device access data that different rates. The buffer provides a waiting station where data can rest while the slower device catches up. Fig 2.3 shows the spooling.

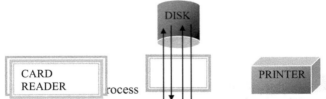

- Computer can perform I/O in parallel with computation, it becomes possible to have the computer read a deck of cards to a tape, drum or disk and to write out to a tape printer while it was computing. This process is called spooling.

- The most common spooling application is print spooling. In print spooling, documents are loaded into a buffer and then the printer pulls them off the buffer at its own rate.
- Spooling is also used for processing data at remote sites. The CPU sends the data via communications path to a remote printer. Spooling overlaps the I/O of one job with the computation of other jobs.
- One difficulty with simple batch systems is that the computer still needs to read the decks of cards before it can begin to execute the job. This means that the CPU is idle during these relatively slow operations.
- Spooling batch systems were the first and are the simplest of the multiprogramming systems.

Advantage of Spooling
1. The spooling operation uses a disk as a very large buffer.
2. Spooling is however capable of overlapping I/O operation for one job with processor operations for another job.

2.8 Essential Properties of the Operating System

1. Batch : Jobs with similar needs are batched together and run through the computer as a group by an operator or automatic job sequencer. Performance is increased by attempting to keep CPU and I/O devices busy at all times through buffering , off line operation, spooling and multiprogramming. A Batch system is good for executing large jobs that need little interaction, it can be submitted and picked up latter.

2. Time sharing : Uses CPU s scheduling and multiprogramming to provide economical interactive use of a system. The CPU switches rapidly from one user to another i.e. the CPU is shared between a number of interactive users. Instead of having a job defined by spooled card images, each program reads its next control instructions from the terminal and output is normally printed immediately on the screen.

3. Interactive : User is on line with computer system and interacts with it via an interface. It is typically composed of many short transactions where the result of the next transaction may be unpredictable. Response time needs to be short since the user submits and waits for the result.

4. Real time system : Real time systems are usually dedicated, embedded systems. They typically read from and react to sensor data. The system must guarantee response to events within fixed periods of time to ensure correct performance.
5. Distributed : Distributes computation among several physical processors. The processors do not share memory or a clock. Instead, each processor has its own local memory. They communicate with each other through various communication lines.

2.9 Summary

An **operating system** provides services to programs and to the users of those programs. It provided by one environment for the execution of programs. The services provided by one operating system is difficult than other operating system. Operating system makes the programming task easier.

Batch operating system is one where programs and data are collected together in a batch before processing starts. In batch operating system memory is usually divided into two areas : Operating system and user program area.

Time sharing, or multitasking, is a logical extension of multiprogramming. Multiple jobs are executed by the CPU switching between them, but the switches occur so frequently that the users may interact with each program while it is running.

When two or more programs are in memory at the same time, sharing the processor is referred to the **multiprogramming operating system.**

Spooling is useful because device access data that different rates. The buffer provides a waiting station where data can rest while the slower device catches up.

2.10 Model Question

Q. 1 Explain various operating system services?

Q. 2 Define Spooling? Describe Spooling process?

Q. 3 Differentiate Multitasking & Multiprogramming?

CHAPTER 3
PROCESS MANAGEMENT

Unit Structure
3.0 Objectives
3.1 Concept of Process
    3.1.1 Processes and Programs
3.2 Process State
    3.2.1 Suspended Processes
    3.2.2 Process Control Block
3.3 Process Management
    3.3.1 Scheduling Queues
    3.3.2 Schedulers

3.4 Context Switching
3.5 Operation on processes
3.6 Co-operating Processes
3.7 Summary
3.8 Model Question

3.0 Objectives

After going through this unit, you will be able to:

- To introduce the notion of a process – a program in execution, which forms the basis of all computation

- To describe the various features of processes, including scheduling, creation and termination, and communication.

3.1 Concept of Process

- A process is sequential program in execution. A process defines the fundamental unit of computation for the computer. Components of process are :
1. Object Program
2. Data
3. Resources
4. Status of the process execution.
- Object program i.e. code to be executed. Data is used for executing the program. While executing the program, it may require some resources. Last component is used for verifying the status of the process execution. A process can run to completion only when all requested resources have been allocated to the process. Two or more processes could be executing the same program, each using their own data and resources.

3.1.1 Processes and Programs

- Process is a dynamic entity, that is a program in execution. A process is a sequence of information executions. Process exists in a limited span of time. Two or more processes could be executing the same program, each using their own data and resources.
- Program is a static entity made up of program statement. Program contains the instructions. A program exists at single place in space and continues to exist. A program does not perform the action by itself.

3.2 Process State

- When process executes, it changes state. Process state is defined as the current activity of the process. Fig. 3.1 shows the general form of the process state transition diagram. Process state contains five states. Each process is in one of the states. The states are listed below.
1. New
2. Ready
3. Running
4. Waiting
5. Terminated(exist)

1. New : A process that just been created.
2. Ready : Ready processes are waiting to have the processor allocated to them by the operating system so that they can run.
3. Running : The process that is currently being executed. A running process possesses all the resources needed for its execution, including the processor.
4. Waiting : A process that can not execute until some event occurs such as the completion of an I/O operation. The running process may become suspended by invoking an I/O module.
5. Terminated : A process that has been released from the pool of executable processes by the operating system.

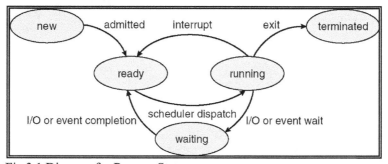
Fig 3.1 Diagram for Process State

- Whenever processes changes state, the operating system reacts by placing the process PCB in the list that corresponds to its new state. Only one process can be running on any processor at any instant and many processes may be ready and waiting state.

3.2.1 Suspended Processes

Characteristics of suspend process

1. Suspended process is not immediately available for execution.
2. The process may or may not be waiting on an event.
3. For preventing the execution, process is suspend by OS, parent process, process itself and an agent.
4. Process may not be removed from the suspended state until the agent orders the removal.

- Swapping is used to move all of a process from main memory to disk. When all the process by putting it in the suspended state and transferring it to disk.

Reasons for process suspension

1. Swapping
2. Timing
3. Interactive user request
4. Parent process request

Swapping : OS needs to release required main memory to bring in a process that is ready to execute.

Timing : Process may be suspended while waiting for the next time interval.

Interactive user request : Process may be suspended for debugging purpose by user.

Parent process request : To modify the suspended process or to coordinate the activity of various descendants.

3.2.2 Process Control Block (PCB)

- Each process contains the process control block (PCB). PCB is the data structure used by the operating system. Operating system groups all information that needs about particular process. Fig. 3.2 shows the process control block.

Pointer	Process State
Process Number	
Program Counter	
CPU registers	
Memory Allocation	
Event Information	
List of open files	

Fig. 3.2 Process Control Block

1. Pointer : Pointer points to another process control block. Pointer is used for maintaining the scheduling list.
2. Process State : Process state may be new, ready, running, waiting and so on.
3. Program Counter : It indicates the address of the next instruction to be executed for this process.
4. Event information : For a process in the blocked state this field contains information concerning the event for which the process is waiting.
5. CPU register : It indicates general purpose register, stack pointers, index registers and accumulators etc. number of register and type of register totally depends upon the computer architecture.
6. Memory Management Information : This information may include the value of base and limit register. This information is useful for deallocating the memory when the process terminates.
7. Accounting Information : This information includes the amount of CPU and real time used, time limits, job or process numbers, account numbers etc.
- Process control block also includes the information about CPU scheduling, I/O resource management, file management information, priority and so on.

The PCB simply serves as the repository for any information that may vary from process to process.

- When a process is created, hardware registers and flags are set to the values provided by the loader or linker. Whenever that process is suspended, the contents of the processor register are usually saved on the stack and the pointer to the related stack frame is stored in the PCB. In this way, the hardware state can be restored when the process is scheduled to run again.

3.3 Process Management / Process Scheduling

- Multiprogramming operating system allows more than one process to be loaded into the executable memory at a time and for the loaded process to share the CPU using time multiplexing.
- The scheduling mechanism is the part of the process manager that handles the removal of the running process from the CPU and the selection of another process on the basis of particular strategy.

3.3.1 Scheduling Queues

- When the process enters into the system, they are put into a job queue. This queue consists of all processes in the system. The operating system also has other queues.
- Device queue is a queue for which a list of processes waiting for a particular I/O device. Each device has its own device queue. Fig. 3.3 shows the queuing diagram of process scheduling. In the fig 3.3, queue is represented

by rectangular box. The circles represent the resources that serve the queues. The arrows indicate the flow of processes in the system.

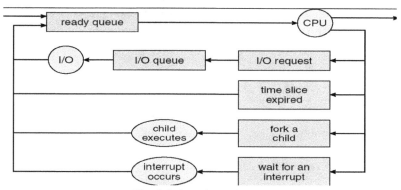

Fig. 3.3 Queuing Diagram

- Queues are of two types : ready queue and set of device queues. A newly arrived process is put in the ready queue. Processes are waiting in ready queue for allocating the CPU. Once the CPU is assigned to the process, then process will execute. While executing the process, one of the several events could occur.
  1. The process could issue an I/O request and then place in an I/O queue.
  2. The process could create new sub process and waits for its termination.
  3. The process could be removed forcibly from the CPU, as a result of interrupt and put back in the ready queue.

3.3.1.1 Two State Process Model
- Process may be in one of two states :
a) Running
b) Not Running

- when new process is created by OS, that process enters into the system in the running state.

- Processes that are not running are kept in queue, waiting their turn to execute. Each entry in the queue is a printer to a particular process. Queue is implemented by using linked list. Use of dispatcher is as follows. When a process interrupted, that process is transferred in the waiting queue. If the process has completed or aborted, the process is discarded. In either case, the dispatcher then select a process from the queue to execute.

3.3.2 Schedules
- Schedulers are of three types.
1. Long Term Scheduler
2. Short Term Scheduler
3. Medium Term Scheduler

3.2.2.1 Long Term Scheduler
- It is also called job scheduler. Long term scheduler determines which programs are admitted to the system for processing. Job scheduler selects processes from the queue and loads them into memory for execution. Process loads into the memory for CPU scheduler. The primary objective of the job scheduler is to provide a balanced mix of jobs, such as I/O bound and processor bound. It also controls the degree of multiprogramming. If the degree of multiprogramming is stable, then the average rate of process creation must be equal to the average departure rate of processes leaving the system.
- On same systems, the long term scheduler may be absent or minimal. Time-sharing operating systems have no long term scheduler. When process changes the state from new to ready, then there is a long term scheduler.

3.2.2.2 Short Term Scheduler
- It is also called CPU scheduler. Main objective is increasing system performance in accordance with the chosen set of criteria. It is the change of ready state to running state of the process. CPU scheduler selects from among the processes that are ready to execute and allocates the CPU to one of them.

- Short term scheduler also known as dispatcher, execute most frequently and makes the fine grained decision of which process to execute next. Short term scheduler is faster than long term scheduler.

3.2.2.3 Medium Term Scheduler
- Medium term scheduling is part of the swapping function. It removes the processes from the memory. It reduces the degree of multiprogramming. The medium term scheduler is in charge of handling the swapped out-processes.

Medium term scheduler is shown in the Fig. 3.4

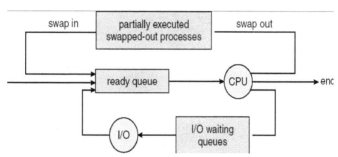

Fig 3.4 Queueing diagram with medium term scheduler

Running process may become suspended by making an I/O request. Suspended processes cannot make any progress towards completion. In this condition, to remove the process from memory and make space for other process. Suspended process is move to the secondary storage is called swapping, and the process is said to be swapped out or rolled out. Swapping may be necessary to improve the process mix.

3.2.2.4 Comparison between Scheduler

Sr. No.	Long Term	Short Term	Medium Term
1	It is job scheduler	It is CPU Scheduler	It is swapping
2	Speed is less than short term scheduler	Speed is very fast	Speed is in between both
3	It controls degree of multiprogramming	Less control over degree of multiprogramming	Reduce the degree of multiprogramming.
4	Absent or minimal in time sharing system.	Minimal in time sharing system.	Time sharing system use medium term scheduler.
5	It select processes from pool and load them into memory for execution.	It select from among the processes that are ready to execute.	Process can be reintroduced into memory and its execution can be continued.
6	Process state is (New to Ready)	Process state is (Ready to Running)	-
7	Select a good process, mix of I/O bound and CPU bound.	Select a new process for a CPU quite frequently.	-

3.4 Context Switch

- When the scheduler switches the CPU from executing one process to executing another, the context switcher saves the content of all processor registers for the process being removed from the CPU in its process being removed from the CPU in its process descriptor. The context of a process is represented in the process control block of a process. Context switch time is pure overhead. Context switching can significantly affect performance, since modern computers have a lot of general and status registers to be saved.
- Content switch times are highly dependent on hardware support. Context switch requires (n + m) bXK time units to save the state of the processor with n general registers, assuming b store operations are required to save register and each store instruction requires K time units. Some hardware systems employ two or more sets of processor registers to reduce the amount of context switching time.
- When the process is switched the information stored is :
  1. Program Counter
  2. Scheduling Information
  3. Base and limit register value
  4. Currently used register
  5. Changed State
  6. I/O State
  7. Accounting

3.5 Operation on Processes

- Several operations are possible on the process. Process must be created and deleted dynamically. Operating system must provide the environment for the process operation. We discuss the two main operations on processes.
  1. Create a process
  2. Terminate a process

3.5.1 Create Process

- Operating system creates a new process with the specified or default attributes and identifier. A process may create several new subprocesses. Syntax for creating new process is :

CREATE (processed, attributes)

- Two names are used in the process they are parent process and child process. Parent process is a creating process. Child process is created by the parent process. Child process may create another subprocess. So it forms a tree of processes. When operating system issues a CREATE system call, it obtains a new process control block from the pool of free memory, fills the fields with provided and default parameters, and insert the PCB into the ready list. Thus it makes the specified process eligible to run the process.

- When a process is created, it requires some parameters. These are priority, level of privilege, requirement of memory, access right, memory protection information etc. Process will need certain resources, such as CPU time, memory, files and I/O devices to complete the operation. When process creates a subprocess, that subprocess may obtain its resources directly from the operating system. Otherwise it uses the resources of parent process.
- When a process creates a new process, two possibilities exist in terms of execution.
1. The parent continues to execute concurrently with its children.
2. The parent waits until some or all of its children have terminated.
    - For address space, two possibilities occur:
1. The child process is a duplicate of the parent process.
2. The child process has a program loaded into it.

3.5.2 Terminate a Process

- DELETE system call is used for terminating a process. A process may delete itself or by another process. A process can cause the termination of another process via an appropriate system call. The operating system reacts by reclaiming all resources allocated to the specified process, closing files opened by or for the process. PCB is also removed from its place of residence in the list and is returned to the free pool. The DELETE service is normally invoked as a part of orderly program termination.

- Following are the resources for terminating the child process by parent process.
1. The task given to the child is no longer required.
2. Child has exceeded its usage of some of the resources that it has been allocated.
3. Operating system does not allow a child to continue if its parent terminates.

3.6 Co-operating Processes

- Co-operating process is a process that can affect or be affected by the other processes while executing. If suppose any process is sharing data with other processes, then it is called co-operating process. Benefit of the co-operating processes are :
1. Sharing of information
2. Increases computation speed
3. Modularity
4. Convenience
- Co-operating processes share the information : Such as a file, memory etc. System must provide an environment to allow concurrent access to these types of resources. Computation speed will increase if the computer has multiple processing elements are connected together. System is constructed in a modular fashion. System function is divided into number of modules.

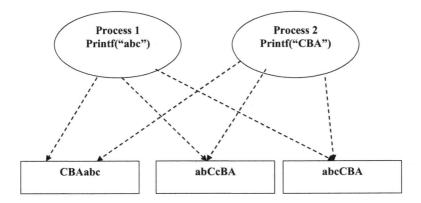

- Behavior of co-operating processes is nondeterministic i.e. it depends on relative execution sequence and cannot be predicted a priori. Co-operating processes are also Reproducible. For example, suppose one process writes "ABC", another writes "CBA" can get different outputs, cannot tell what comes from which. Which process output first "C" in "ABCCBA". The subtle state sharing that occurs here via the terminal. Not just anything can happen, though. For example, "AABBCC" cannot occur.

3.7 Summary

A process is a program in execution. As a process executes, it changes state. The state of a process is defined by that process's current activity. Each process may be in one of the following states: new, ready, running, waiting, or terminated. Each process is represented in the operating system by its own process control block (PCB).

A process, when it is not executing, placed in some waiting queue. There are two major classes of queues in an operating system: I/O request queues and the ready queue. The ready queue contains all the processes that are ready to execute and are waiting for the CPU. Each process is represented by a PCB and the PCBs can be linked together to form a ready queue. Long-term(job) scheduling is the selection of processes that will be allowed to contend for the CPU. Normally, long-term scheduling is heavily influenced by resources-allocation considerations, especially memory management. Short-term(CPU) scheduling is the selection of one process from the ready queue.

Operating systems must provide a mechanism for parent processes to create new child processes. The parent may wait for its children to terminate before proceeding, or the parent and children may execute concurrently. There are several reasons for allowing concurrent execution: information sharing computation speedup, modularity, and convenience.

The processes executing in the operating system may be either independent processes or cooperating processes. Cooperating processes require an inter-process communication mechanism to communicate with each other. Principally, communication is achieved through two schemes: shared memory and message passing. The shared-memory method requires communicating processes through the use of these shared variables. In a shared-memory system, the responsibility for providing communication rests with the application programmers: the operating system needs to provide only the shared memory. The responsibility for providing communication may rest with the operating system itself. These two schemes are not mutually exclusive and can be used simultaneously within a single operating system.

3.8 Model Question

Q.1 Define process and programs?

Q.2 Describe Process Control Block?

Q.3 Explain Scheduling Queues?

Q.4 Explain schedulers and its types?

Q.5 Differentiate various types of scheduler?

Q.6 Explain context switch?

Q.7 Explain operation on processes?

CHAPTER 4

THREAD MANAGEMENT

Unit Structure

4.0 Objectives

4.1 Introduction Of Thread

4.2 Types of Thread

      4.2.1 User Level Thread

      4.2.2 Kernel Level Thread

      4.2.3 Advantage of Thread

4.3 Multithreading Models

      4.3.1 Many to Many Model

      4.3.2 Many to One Model

      4.3.3 One to One Model

4.4 Difference between User Level and Kernel Level Thread

4.5 Difference between Process and Thread

4.6 Threading Issues

4.7 Summary

4.8 Model Question

4.0 Objectives

After going through this unit, you will be able to:

- To introduce Thread & its types, Multithreading Models and Threading issues.

4.1 Introduction of Thread

- A thread is a flow of execution through the process code, with its own program counter, system registers and stack. Threads are a popular way to improve application performance through parallelism. A thread is sometimes called **a light weight process.**
- Threads represent a software approach to improving performance of operating system by reducing the over head thread is equivalent to a classical process. Each thread belongs to exactly one process and no thread

can exist outside a process. Each thread represents a separate flow of control.

- Fig. 4.1shows the single and multithreaded process.

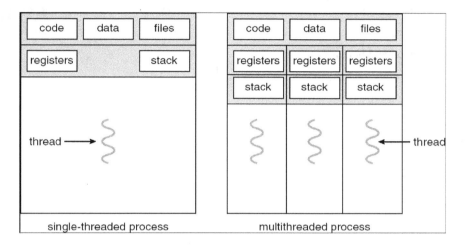

single-threaded process   multithreaded process

- Threads have been successfully used in implementing network servers. They also provide a suitable foundation for parallel execution of applications on shared memory multiprocessors.

4.2 Types of Thread

Threads is implemented in two ways :

1. User Level
2. Kernel Level

4.2.1 User Level Thread

- In a user thread, all of the work of thread management is done by the application and the kernel is not aware of the existence of threads. The thread library contains code for creating and destroying threads, for passing message and data between threads, for scheduling thread execution and for saving and restoring thread contexts. The application begins with a single thread and begins running in that thread.
- Fig. 4.2 shows the user level thread.

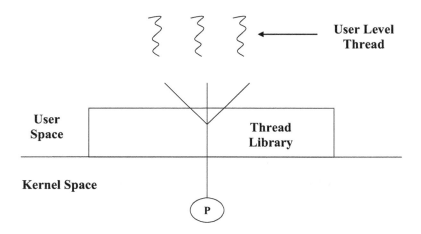

User level threads are generally fast to create and manage.

Advantage of user level thread over Kernel level thread :

1. Thread switching does not require Kernel mode privileges.
2. User level thread can run on any operating system.
3. Scheduling can be application specific.
4. User level threads are fast to create and manage.

Disadvantages of user level thread :

1. In a typical operating system, most system calls are blocking.
2. Multithreaded application cannot take advantage of multiprocessing.

4.2.2 Kernel Level Threads

- In Kernel level thread, thread management done by the Kernel. There is no thread management code in the application area. Kernel threads are supported directly by the operating system. Any application can be programmed to be multithreaded. All of the threads within an application are supported within a single process. The Kernel maintains context information for the process as a whole and for individuals threads within the process.

- Scheduling by the Kernel is done on a thread basis. The Kernel performs thread creation, scheduling and management in Kernel space. Kernel threads are generally slower to create and manage than the user threads.

Advantages of Kernel level thread:

1. Kernel can simultaneously schedule multiple threads from the same process on multiple process.

2. If one thread in a process is blocked, the Kernel can schedule another thread of the same process.

3. Kernel routines themselves can multithreaded.

Disadvantages:

1. Kernel threads are generally slower to create and manage than the user threads.

2. Transfer of control from one thread to another within same process requires a mode switch to the Kernel.

4.2.3 Advantages of Thread

1. Thread minimize context switching time.

2. Use of threads provides concurrency within a process.

3. Efficient communication.

4. Economy- It is more economical to create and context switch threads.

5. Utilization of multiprocessor architectures –

The benefits of multithreading can be greatly increased in a multiprocessor architecture.

4.3 Multithreading Models

- Some operating system provide a combined user level thread and Kernel level thread facility. Solaris is a good example of this combined approach. In a combined system, multiple threads within the same application can run in parallel on multiple processors and a blocking system call need not block the entire process.

- Multithreading models are three types:

1. Many to many relationship.

2. Many to one relationship.

3. One to one relationship.

4.3.1 Many to Many Model

- In this model, many user level threads multiplexes to the Kernel thread of smaller or equal numbers. The number of Kernel threads may be specific to either a particular application or a particular machine.

- Fig. 4.3 shows the many to many model. In this model, developers can create as many user threads as necessary and the corresponding Kernel threads can run in parallels on a multiprocessor.

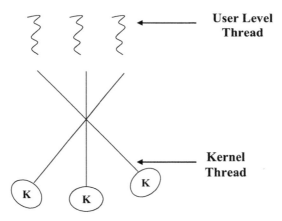

4.3.2 Many to One Model

- Many to one model maps many user level threads to one Kernel level thread. Thread management is done in user space. When thread makes a blocking system call, the entire process will be blocks. Only one thread can access the Kernel at a time, so multiple threads are unable to run in parallel on multiprocessors.

- Fig.4.4 shows the many to one model.

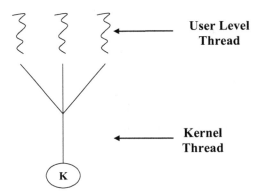

- If the user level thread libraries are implemented in the operating system, that system does not support Kernel threads use the many to one relationship modes.

4.3.3 One to One Model

- There is one to one relationship of user level thread to the kernel level thread. Fig. 4.5 shows one to one relationship model. This model provides more concurrency than the many to one model.

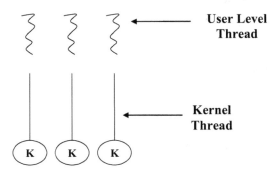

- It also another thread to run when a thread makes a blocking system call. It support multiple thread to execute in parallel on microprocessors. Disadvantage of this model is that creating user thread requires the corresponding Kernel thread. OS/2, windows NT and windows 2000 use one to one relationship model.

4.4 Difference between User Level & Kernel Level Thread

Sr. No	User Level Threads	Kernel Level Thread
1	User level thread are faster to create and manage.	Kernel level thread are slower to create and manage.
2	Implemented by a thread library at the user level.	Operating system support directly to Kernel threads.
3	User level thread can run on any operating system.	Kernel level threads are specific to the operating system.
4	Support provided at the user level called user level thread.	Support may be provided by kernel is called Kernel level threads.
5	Multithread application cannot take advantage of multiprocessing.	Kernel routines themselves can be multithreaded.

4.5 Difference between Process and Thread

Sr. No	Process	Thread
1	Process is called heavy weight process.	Thread is called light weight process.
2	Process switching needs interface with operating system.	Thread switching does not need to call a operating system and cause an interrupt to the Kernel.
3	In multiple process implementation each process executes the same code but has its own memory and file resources.	All threads can share same set of open files, child processes.
4	If one server process is blocked no other server process can execute until the first process unblocked.	While one server thread is blocked and waiting, second thread in the same task could run.
5	Multiple redundant process uses more resources than multiple threaded.	Multiple threaded process uses fewer resources than multiple redundant process.
6	In multiple process each process operates independently of the others.	One thread can read, write or even completely wipe out another threads stack.

4.6 Threading Issues

- System calls fork and exec is discussed here. In a multithreaded program environment, fork and exec system calls is changed. Unix system have two version of fork system calls. One call duplicates all threads and another that duplicates only the thread that invoke the fork system call. Whether to use one or two version of fork system call totally depends upon the application. Duplicating all threads is unnecessary, if exec is called immediately after fork system call.

- Thread cancellation is a process of thread terminates before its completion of task. For example, in multiple thread environment, thread concurrently searching through a database. If any one thread returns the result, the remaining thread might be cancelled.

- Thread cancellation is of two types.

1. Asynchronous cancellation

2. Synchronous cancellation

- In asynchronous cancellation, one thread immediately terminates the target thread. Deferred cancellation periodically check for terminate by target thread. It also allow the target thread to terminate itself in an orderly fashion. Some resources are allocated to the thread. If we cancel the thread, which update the data with other thread. This problem may face by asynchronous cancellation system wide resource are not free if threads cancelled asynchronously. Most of the operating system allow a process or thread to be cancelled asynchronously.

4.7 Summary

A thread is a flow of control within a process. A multithreaded process contains several different flows of control within the same address space. The benefits of multithreading include increased responsiveness to the user, resource sharing within the process, economy, and scalability issues such as more efficient use of multiple core.

User level threads are threads are visible to the programmer and are unknown to the kernel. The operating system kernel supports and manages kernel level threads. In general, user level threads are faster to create and manage than are kernel threads, as no intervention from the kernel is required. Three different types of models relate user and kernel threads: the many-to-one model maps many user threads to a single thread. The one to one model maps each user thread to a corresponding kernel thread. The many to many model multiplexers many user threads to a smaller or equal number of kernel threads.

4.8 Model Question

Q. 1 Define thread and its types in detail?

Q. 2 Differentiate user level thread and kernel level thread?

Q. 3 Explain various Multithreaded Model?

Q. 4 Differentiate process and thread?

CHAPTER 5
CONCURRENCY CONTROL

Unit Structure

5.0 Objectives

5.0 Objectives

After going through this unit, you will be able to:

- To introduce the concurrency control and Race condition, critical section problem, where solutions can be used to ensure the consistency of shared data.
- To present both software and hardware solutions of the critical section problem.

5.1 Principle of Concurrency

In a single-processor multiprogramming system, processes are interleaved in time to yield the appearance of simultaneous execution. Even parallel processing is not achieved, and ever though there is a certain amount of overhead involved in switching back and forth between processes, interleaved execution provides major benefits in processing efficiency and in program structuring. In a multiple processor system, it is possible not only to interleave the execution of multiple processes but also to overlap them. It is assumed, it may seem that interleaving and overlapping represent fundamentally different modes of execution and present different problems. In fact, both techniques can be viewed as examples of concurrent processing, and both present the same problems. The relative speed of execution of processes It depends on activities of other processes, the way in which the operating system handles interrupts, and the scheduling policies of the operating, system.

There are quite difficulties:

1. The sharing of global resources. For example, if two processes both make use of the same global variable and both perform reads and writes on that variable, then the order in which the various reads and writes are executed is critical.

2. It is difficult for the operating system to manage the allocation of resources optimally.

3. It is very difficult to locate a programming error because results are typically not deterministic and reproducible.

Eg:

```
Void echo()
{
chin = getchar();
chout = chin;
putchar(chout);
}
```

This procedure shows the essential elements of a program that will provide a character echo procedure; input is obtained from a keyboard one keystroke at a time. Each input character is stored in variable chin. It is then transferred to variable chout and sent to the display. Any program can call this procedure repeatedly to accept user input and display it on the user's screen.

In a single - processor multiprogramming system supporting a single user. The user can jump from one application to another, and each .application uses the same keyboard for input and the same screen for output. Because each application needs to use the procedure echo, it makes sense for it to be a shared procedure that is loaded into a portion of memory global to all applications. Thus, only a single copy of the echo procedure is used, saving space.

The sharing of main memory among processes is useful to permit efficient and close interaction among processes Consider the following sequence:

1. Process P1 invokes the echo procedure and is interrupted immediately after getchar returns its value and stores it in chin. At this point, the most recently entered character, x, is stored in variable chin.

2. Process P2 is activated and invokes the echo procedure, which runs to conclusion, inputting and then displaying a single character, y, on the screen.

3. Process P1 is resumed. By this time, the value x has been overwritten in chin and therefore lost. Instead, chin contains y, which is transferred to chout and displayed.

Thus, the first character is lost and the second character is displayed twice. Because of shared global variable, chin. If one process updates the global variable and then is interrupted, another .process may alter the variable before the first process can use its value. However, if only one process at a time may be in that procedure. Then the foregoing sequence would result in the following:

1. Process P1 invokes the echo procedure and is interrupted immediately after the conclusion of the input function. At this point, the most recently entered character, x, is stored in variable chin.

2. Process P2 is activated and invokes the echo procedure. However, because P1 is still inside the echo procedure, although currently suspended, P2 is blocked from entering the procedure. Therefore, P2 is suspended awaiting the availability of the echo procedure.

3. At some later time, process PI is resumed and completes execution of echo. The proper character, x, is displayed.

4. When PI exits' echo, this removes the block on P2. When P2 is later resumed, the echo procedure is successfully invoked.

Therefore it is necessary to protect shared global variables. And that the only way to do that is to control the code that accesses the variable.

5.2 Race Condition

A race condition occurs when multiple processes or threads read and write data items so that the final result depends on the order of execution of instructions in the multiple processes.

Suppose that two processes, P1 and P2, share the global variable a. At some point in its execution, P1 updates a to the value 1, and at some point in its execution, P2 updates a to the value 2. Thus, the two tasks are in a race to write variable a. In this example the "loser" of the race (the process that updates last) determines the final value of a.

Therefore Operating System Concerns of following things
1. The operating system must be able to keep track of the various processes
2. The operating system must allocate and deallocate various resources for each active process.
3. The operating system must protect the data and physical resources of each process against unintended interference by other processes.

4. The functioning of a process, and the output it produces, must be independent of the speed at which its execution is carried out relative to the speed of other concurrent processes.

Process Interaction can be defined as
• Processes unaware of each other
• Processes indirectly aware of each other
• Processes directly aware of each other
     Concurrent processes come into conflict with each other when they are competing for the use of the same resource.
     Two or more processes need to access a resource during the course of their execution. Each process is unaware of the existence of the other processes. There is no exchange of information between the competing processes.

5.3 Requirements for Mutual Exclusion

1. Mutual exclusion must be enforced: Only one process at a time is allowed into its critical section, among all processes that have critical sections for the same resource or shared object.

2. A process that halts in its non critical section must do so without interfering with other processes.

3. It must not be possible for a process requiring access to a critical section to be delayed indefinitely: no deadlock or starvation.

4. When no process is in a critical section, any process that requests entry to its critical section must be permitted to enter without delay.

5. No assumptions are made about relative process speeds or number of processors.

6. A process remains inside its critical section for a finite time only.

5.4 Mutual Exclusion – Software Support

Software approaches can be implemented for concurrent processes that executes on a single processor or a multiprocessor machine with shared main memory.

5.4.1 Dekkers Algorithm

- Dekkers algorithm is for two processes based solely on software. Each of these processes loop indefinitely, repeatedly entering and reentering its critical section. A process (P0 & P1) that wishes to execute its critical section first enters the igloo and examines the blackboard. The process number is written on the blackboard, that process leaves the igloo and proceeds to critical section. Otherwise that process will wait for its turn. Process reenters in the igloo to check the blackboard. It repeats this exercise until it is allowed to enter its critical section. This procedure is known as busy waiting.

- In formal terms, there is a shared global variable : Var turn : 0 : 1;

Process 0

- - - -

- - - -

While turn # 0 do (nothing)
<critical section>;
turn := 1;

- - - -

Process 1

- - - -

- - - -

While turn # 1 do (nothing);
<critical section>;
Turn := 0;

\- - - -

- The above solution satisfy the property of mutual exclusion. Drawback of the solution are as follows:

1. Processes must strictly alternate in their use of their critical section.

2. if one process fails, the other process is permanently blocked.

Drawbacks of software solutions

1. Complicated to program.

2. busy waiting is possible.

3. it would be more efficient to block processes that are waiting.

4. makes difficult assumptions about the memory system.

5.5 Mutual Exclusion – Hardware Support

Hardware approaches to mutual exclusion.

5.5.1 Interrupt Disabling:

In a uniprocessor machine, concurrent processes cannot be overlapped; they can only be interleaved. Furthermore, a process will continue to run until it invokes an operating system service or until it is interrupted. Therefore, to guarantee mutual exclusion, it is sufficient to prevent a process from being interrupted. This capability can be provided in the form of primitives defined by the system kernel for disabling and enabling interrupts.

```
eg:
while (true)
(
disable interrupts()
critical section
enable interrupts()
) remainder
```

Because the critical section cannot be interrupted, mutual exclusion is guaranteed.
Disadvantages
- It works only in a single processor environment.

- Interrupts can be lost if not serviced promptly.
- A process waiting to enter its critical section could suffer from starvation.

5.5.2 Test and Set Instruction

- It is special machine instruction used to avoid mutual exclusion. The test and set instruction can be defined as follows:

boolean testset (int i)
{
    if (i==o)
{
i=1;
    return true;
}
else., .
{
    return false;
}

The above function is carried out automatically.

Advantages
1. It is simple and easy to verify.
2. it is applicable to any number of processes.
3. it can b used to support multiple critical section.

Disadvantages
1. Busy waiting is possible.
2. Starvation is also possible.
3. There may be deadlock.

5.6 Semaphores

- The solutions of the critical section problem represented in the section is not easy to generalize to more complex problems. To overcome this difficulty, we can use a synchronization tool call a semaphore. A semaphore S is an integer variable that, a part from initialization, is a accessed two standard atomic operations: wait and signal. This operations were originally termed P (for wait;from the Dutch proberen, to test) and V (for signal ; from verhogen, to increment).

- The Classical definition of wait and signal are

Wait (S)

{

while (S <=0)

S =S – 1;

}

signal(S)

{

S = S + 1;

}

- The integer value of the semaphore in the wait and signal operations must be executed indivisibly. That is, when one process modifies the semaphore value, no other process can simultaneously modify that same semaphore value.
- In addition, in the case of the wait(S), the testing of the integer value of S (S 0), and its possible modification (S := S – 1), must also be executed without interruption.
- Semaphores are not provided by hardware. But they have several attractive properties:

1. Semaphores are machine independent.
2. Semaphores are simple to implement.
3. Correctness is easy to determine.
4. Can have many different critical sections with different semaphores.
5. Semaphore acquire many resources simultaneously.

Drawback of Semaphore

1. They are essentially shared global variables.

2. Access to semaphores can come from anywhere in a program.

3. There is no control or guarantee of proper usage.

4. There is no linguistic connection between the semaphore and the data to which the semaphore controls access.

5. They serve two purposes, mutual exclusion and scheduling constraints.

5.7 Monitors

- The monitor is a programming-language construct that provides equivalent functionality to that of semaphores and that is easier to control. The monitor construct has been implemented in a number of programming languages, including Concurrent Pascal, Pascal-Plus, Modula-2, Modula-3, and Java. It has also been implemented as a program library. This allows programmers to put monitor locks on any object.

Monitor with Signal

- A monitor is a software module consisting of one or more procedures, an initialization sequence, and local data The characteristics of a monitor are the following:

1. The local data variables are accessible only by the monitor's procedures and not by any external procedure.

2. A process enters the monitor by invoking one of its procedures.

3. Only one process may De executing in the monitor at a time; any other process that has invoked the monitor is blocked, waiting for the monitor to become available.

A monitor supports synchronization by the use of **condition variables** that are contained Within the monitor and accessible only within the monitor. Condition variables are a special data type in monitors, which are operated on by two functions:

• cwait (c): Suspend execution of the calling process on condition c. The monitor is now available for use by another process.

• csignal (c): Resume execution of some process blocked after a cwait on the same condition)lf there are several such processes, choose one of them; if there is no such process, do nothing.

- Monitor wait and signal operations are different from those for the semaphore. If a process in a monitor signals and no task is waiting on the condition variable, the signal is lost.
- Although a process can enter the monitor by invoking any of its procedures, we can think of the monitor as having a single entry point that is guarded so that only one process may be in the monitor at a time. Other processes that attempt to enter the monitor join a queue of processes blocked waiting for monitor availability.
- Once a process is in the monitor, it may temporarily block itself on condition x by issuing cwait (x); it is then placed in a queue of processes waiting to reenter the monitor when the condition changes, and resume execution at the point in its program following the cwait (x) call.
- If a process that is executing in the monitor detects a change in condition variable x, it issues csignal (x), which alerts the corresponding condition queue that the condition has changed.
- A producer can add characters to the buffer only by means of the procedure append inside the monitor; the producer does not have direct access to buffer.
- The procedure first-checks the condition not full to determine if there is space available in the buffer. If not, the process executing the monitor is blocked on that condition.

5.7 Summary

Critical section is a code that only one process at a time can be executing. Critical section problem is design an algorithm that allows at most one process into the critical section at a time, without deadlock. Solution of the critical section problem must satisfy mutual exclusion, progress, bounded waiting.

Semaphore is a synchronization variable that tasks on positive integer values. Binary semaphore are those that have only two values 0 and 1. semaphores are not provided by hardware. Semaphore is used to solve critical section problem.

A monitor is a software module consisting of one or more procedures, an initialization sequence and local data. Components of monitors are shared data declaration, shared data initialization, operations on shared data and synchronization statement.

5.8 Model Question

Q.1   Explain in brief race condition?

Q.2   Define the term critical section?

Q.3   What are the requirement for critical section problem?

Q.4   Write a short note on:

a) Semaphore

b) Monitors

Q.5   What are semaphores? How do they implement mutual exclusion?

Q.6   Describe hardware solution to the critical section problem?

CHAPTER 6
DEADLOCK

Unit Structure
6.0 Objectives

6.1 Introduction

6.2 Deadlock Characterization

6.0 Objectives

After going through this unit, you will be able to:

- To develop a description of deadlocks, which prevent sets of concurrent processes from completing their tasks.
- To present number of different methods for preventing or avoiding deadlocks in a computer system.

6.1 Introduction

In a multiprogramming environment, several processes may compete for a finite number of resources. A process requests resources; if the resources are not available at that time, the process enters a wait state. It may happen that waiting processes will never again change state, because the resources they have requested are held by other waiting processes. This situation is called deadlock.

If a process requests an instance of a resource type, the allocation of any instance of the type will satisfy the request. If it will not, then the instances are not identical, and the resource type classes have not been defined properly.

A process must request a resource before using it, and must release the resource after using it. A process may request as many resources as it requires to carry out its designated task.

Under the normal mode of operation, a process may utilize a resource in only the following sequence:

1. **Request**: If the request cannot be granted immediately, then the requesting process must wait until it can acquire the resource.

2. **Use:** The process can operate on the resource.

3. **Release**: The process releases the resource

6.2 Deadlock Characterization

In deadlock, processes never finish executing and system resources are tied up, preventing other jobs from ever starting.

Necessary Conditions

A deadlock situation can arise if the following four conditions hold simultaneously in a system:

1. **Mutual exclusion:** At least one resource must be held in a non-sharable mode; that is, only one process at a time can use the resource. If another process requests that resource, the requesting process must be delayed until the resource has been released.

2. **Hold and wait :** There must exist a process that is holding at least one resource and is waiting to acquire additional resources that are currently being held by other processes.

3. **No preemption** : Resources cannot be preempted; that is, a resource can be released only voluntarily by the process holding it, after that process, has completed its task.

4. **Circular wait:** There must exist a set {P0, P1, ..., Pn } of waiting processes such that P0 is waiting for a resource that is held by P1, P1 is waiting for a resource that is held by P2, ..., Pn-1 is waiting for a resource that is held by Pn, and Pn is waiting for a resource that is held by P0.

6.2.1 Resource-Allocation Graph

Deadlocks can be described more precisely in terms of a directed graph called a system resource-allocation graph. The set of vertices V is partitioned into two different types of nodes P = {P1, P2, ... Pn} the set consisting of all the active processes in the system; and R = {R1, R2, ..., R1}, the set consisting of all resource types in the system.

A directed edge from process Pi to resource type Rj is denoted by Pi → Rj, it signifies that process Pi requested an instance of resource type Rj and is currently waiting for that resource. A directed edge from resource type Rj toprocess Pi is denoted by Rj_ Pi it signifies that an instance of resource type Rj has been allocated to process Pi. A directed edge Pi_ Rj is called a request edge; a directed edge Rj _ Pi is called an assignment edge.

When process Pi requests an instance of resource type Rj, a request edge is inserted in the resource-allocation graph. When this request can be fulfilled, the request edge is instantaneously transformed to an assignment edge. When the process no longer needs access to the, resource it releases the resource, and as a result the assignment edge is deleted.

Definition of a resource-allocation graph, it can be shown that, if the graph contains no cycles, then no process in the system is deadlocked. If, on the other hand, the graph contains the cycle, then a deadlock must exist.

If each resource type has several instances, then a cycle implies that a deadlock has occurred. If the cycle involves only a set of resources types, each of which has only a single instance, then a deadlock has occurred. Each process involved in the cycle is deadlocked. In this case, a cycle in the graph is both a necessary and a sufficient condition for the existence of deadlock.

A set of vertices V and a set of edges E.

- V is partitioned into two types:
  - $P = \{P1, P2, ..., Pn\}$, the set consisting of all the processes in the system.
  - $R = \{R1, R2, ..., Rm\}$, the set consisting of all resource types in the system.
- request edge – directed edge $P1 \rightarrow Rj$
- assignment edge – directed edge $Rj \rightarrow Pi$

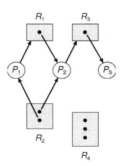

Fig. Resource Allocation Graph

If each resource type has several instance, then a cycle does not necessarily imply that a deadlock incurred. In this case, a cycle in the graph is a necessary but not a sufficient condition for the existence of deadlock.

Suppose that process P3requests an instance of resource type R2 Since no resource instance is currently available, a request edge P3 → R2 is added to the graph. At this point, two minimal cycles exist in the system:

P1 → R1 → P2 → R3 → P3 → R2 → P1

P2 → R3 → P3 → R2 → P2

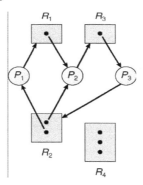

Fig. Resource Allocation Graph with Deadlock

Processes P1, P2, and P3 are deadlocked. Process P2 is waiting for the resource R3, which is held by process P3. Process P3, on the other hand, is waiting for either process P1 or process P2 to release resource R2. In addition, process PI is waiting for process P2 to release resource R1.

6.3 Method For Handling Deadlock //Detection

There are are three different methods for dealing with the deadlock problem:

• We can use a protocol to ensure that the system will never enter a deadlock state.

• We can allow the system to enter a deadlock state and then recover.

• We can ignore the problem all together, and pretend that deadlocks never occur in the system. This solution is the one used by most operating systems, including UNIX.

Deadlock avoidance, on the other hand, requires that the operating system be given in advance additional information concerning which resources a process will request and use during its lifetime. With this additional knowledge, we can decide for each request whether or not the process should wait. Each request requires that the system consider the resources currently available, the resources currently allocated to each process, and the future requests and releases of each process, to decide whether the current request can be satisfied or must be delayed.

If a system does not employ either a deadlock-prevention or a deadlock avoidance algorithm, then a deadlock situation may occur If a system does not ensure that a deadlock will never occur, and also does not provide a mechanism for deadlock detection and recovery, then we may arrive at a situation where the system is in a deadlock state yet has no way of recognizing what has happened.

6.4 Deadlock Prevention

For a deadlock to occur, each of the four necessary-conditions must hold. By ensuring that at least on one these conditions cannot hold, we can prevent the occurrence of a deadlock.

6.4.1 Mutual Exclusion

The mutual-exclusion condition must hold for non-sharable resources. For example, a printer cannot be simultaneously shared by several processes. Sharable resources, on the other hand, do not require mutually exclusive access, and thus cannot be involved in a deadlock.

6.4.2 Hold and Wait

1. When whenever a process requests a resource, it does not hold any other resources. One protocol that be used requires each process to request and be allocated all its resources before it begins execution.

2. An alternative protocol allows a process to request resources only when the process has none. A process may request some resources and use them. Before it can request any additional resources, however it must release all the resources that it is currently allocated here are two main disadvantages to these protocols. First, resource utilization may be low, since many of the resources may be allocated but unused for a long period. In the example given, for instance, we can release the tape drive and disk file, and then again request the disk file and printer, only if we can be sure that our data will remain on the disk file. If we cannot be assured that they will, then we must request all resources at the beginning for both protocols.

Second, starvation is possible.

6.4.3 No Preemption

If a process that is holding some resources requests another resource that cannot be immediately allocated to it, then all resources currently being held are preempted. That is this resources are implicitly released. The preempted resources are added to the list of resources for which the process is waiting process will be restarted only when it can regain its old resources, as well as the new ones that it is requesting.

6.4.4 Circular Wait

Circular-wait condition never holds is to impose a total ordering of all resource types, and to require that each process requests resources in an increasing order of enumeration.

Let $R = \{R1, R2, ..., Rn\}$ be the set of resource types. We assign to each resource type a unique integer number, which allows us to compare two resources and to determine whether one precedes another in our ordering. Formally, we define a one-to-one function $F: R \_ N$, where N is the set of natural numbers.

6.5 Deadlock Avoidance

Prevent deadlocks requests can be made. The restraints ensure that at least one of the necessary conditions for deadlock cannot occur, and, hence, that deadlocks cannot hold. Possible side effects of preventing deadlocks by this, melted, however, are Tow device utilization and reduced system throughput.

An alternative method for avoiding deadlocks is to require additional information about how resources are to be requested. For example, in a system with one tape drive and one printer, we might be told that process P will request first the tape drive, and later the printer, before releasing both resources. Process Q on the other hand, will request first the printer, and then the tape drive. With this knowledge of the complete sequence of requests and releases for each process we can decide for each request whether or not the process should wait.

A deadlock-avoidance algorithm dynamically examines the resource-allocation state to ensure that there can never be a circular wait condition. The resource allocation state is defined by the number of available and allocated resources, and the maximum demands of the processes.

6.5.1 Safe State

A state is safe if the system can allocate resources to each process (up to its maximum) in some order and still avoid a deadlock. More formally, a system is in a safe state only if there exists a safe sequence. A sequence of processes <P1, P2, .. Pn> is a safe sequence for the current allocation state if, for each Pi the resources that Pj can still request can be satisfied by the currently available resources plus the resources held by all the Pj, with j < i. In this situation, if the resources that process Pi needs are not immediately available, then Pi can wait until all Pj have finished. When they have finished, Pi can obtain all of its needed resources, complete its designated task return its allocated resources, and terminate. When Pi terminates, Pi + 1 can obtain its needed resources, and so on.

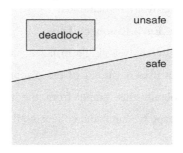

Fig. Safe, Unsafe & Deadlock State

If no such sequence exists, then the system state is said to be unsafe.

6.5.2 Resource-Allocation Graph Algorithm

Suppose that process Pi requests resource Rj. The request can be granted only if converting the request edge Pi → Rj to an assignment edge Rj → Pi does not result in the formation of a cycle in the resource-allocation graph.

6.5.3 Banker's Algorithm

The resource-allocation graph algorithm is not applicable to a resource-allocation system with multiple instances of each resource type. The deadlock-avoidance algorithm that we describe next is applicable to such a system, but is less efficient than the resource-allocation graph scheme. This algorithm is commonly known as the banker's algorithm.

6.6 Deadlock Detection

If a system does not employ either a deadlock-prevention or a deadlock avoidance algorithm, then a deadlock situation may occur.

• An algorithm that examines the state of the system to determine whether a deadlock has occurred.

• An algorithm to recover from the deadlock.

6.6.1 Single Instance of Each Resource Type

If all resources have only a single instance, then we can define a deadlock detection algorithm that uses a variant of the resource-allocation graph, called a wait-for graph. We obtain this graph from the resource-allocation graph by removing the nodes of type resource and collapsing the appropriate edges.

6.6.2 Several Instances of a Resource Type

The wait-for graph scheme is not applicable to a resource-allocation system with multiple instances of each resource type.

The algorithm used are :

• **Available**: A vector of length m indicates the number of available resources of each type.

• **Allocation**: An n x m matrix defines the number of resources of each type currently allocated to each process.

• **Request**: An n x m matrix indicates the current request of each process. If Request [i, j] = k, then process P, is requesting k more instances of resource type Rj.

6.6.3 Detection-Algorithm Usage

If deadlocks occur frequently, then the detection algorithm should be invoked frequently. Resources allocated to deadlocked processes will be idle until the deadlock can be broken.

6.7 Recovery from Deadlock

When a detection algorithm determines that a deadlock exists, several alternatives exist. One possibility is to inform the operator that a deadlock has spurred, and to let the operator deal with the deadlock manually. The other possibility is to let the system recover from the deadlock automatically. There are two options for breaking a deadlock. One solution is simply to abort one or more processes to break the circular wait. The second option is to preempt some resources from one or more of the deadlocked processes.

6.7.1 Process Termination

To eliminate deadlocks by aborting a process, we use one of two methods. In both methods, the system reclaims all resources allocated to the terminated processes.

• **Abort all deadlocked processes**: This method clearly will break the dead – lock cycle, but at a great expense, since these processes may have computed for a long time, and the results of these partial computations must be discarded, and probably must be recomputed.

• **Abort one process at a time until the deadlock cycle is eliminated:** This method incurs considerable overhead, since after each process is aborted a deadlock-detection algorithm must be invoked to determine whether a processes are still deadlocked.

6.7.2 Resource Preemption

To eliminate deadlocks using resource preemption, we successively preempt some resources from processes and give these resources to other processes until he deadlock cycle is broken.

The three issues are considered to recover from deadlock

1. **Selecting a victim**
2. **Rollback**
3. **Starvation**

6.8 Summary

A deadlocked state occurs when two or more processes are waiting indefinitely for an event that can be caused only one of the waiting processes. There are three principal methods for dealing with deadlocks:

- Use some protocol to prevent or avoid deadlocks, entering that the system will never enter a deadlocked state.

- Allow the system to enter a deadlocked state, detect it, and then recover.

- Ignore the problem altogether and pretend that deadlocks never occur in the system.

Deadlock prevention is a set of methods for ensuring that at least one of the necessary condition cannot hold. Deadlock avoidance requires additional information about how resources are to be requested. Deadlock avoidance algorithm dynamically examines the resource allocation state to ensure that a circular wait condition can never exist. Deadlock occur only when some process makes a request that cannot e granted immediately.

6.9 Model Question

Q.1   Write a short note on deadlock?

Q.2   Explain the characteristic of deadlock?

Q.3   Describe various methods for deadlock prevention?

Q.4   Explain the resource allocation graph?

Q.5   Write a note on 'safe state'?

Q.6   Explain how deadlocks are detected and corrected?

Q.7   What are the difference between a deadlock prevention and deadlock Avoidance?

CHAPTER 7
MEMORY MANAGEMENT

Unit Structure

7.0 Objectives

7.1 Introduction

7.2 Memory Partitioning

7.3 Swapping

7.4 Paging

7.5 Segmentation

7.6 Summary

7.7 Model Question

7.1 Objective

- To provide a detailed description of various ways of organizing memory hardware.

- To discuss various memory-management techniques, including paging and segmentation.

- To provide a detailed description of the Intel Pentium, which supports both pure segmentation and segmentation with paging.

7.1 Memory Management

Memory is central to the operation of a modern computer system. Memory is a large array of words or bytes, each with its own address.

A program resides on a disk as a binary executable file. The program must be brought into memory and placed within a process for it to be executed Depending on the memory management in use the process may be moved between disk and memory during its execution. The collection of processes on the disk that are waiting to be brought into memory for execution forms the input queue. i.e. selected one of the process in the input queue and to load that process into memory. We can provide protection by using two registers, usually a base and a limit, as shown in fig. 7.1. the base register holds the smallest legal physical memory address; the limit register specifies the size of the range. For example, if the base register holds 300040 and the limit register is 120900, then the program can legally access all addresses from 300040 through 420939(inclusive).

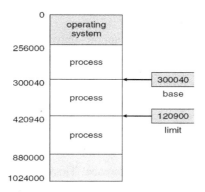

Fig 7.1 A base and limit register define a logical address space.

The binding of instructions and data to memory addresses can be done at any step along the way:

- **Compile time:** If it is known at compile time where the process will reside in memory, then absolute code can be generated.
- **Load time:** If it is not known at compile time where the process will reside in memory, then the compiler must generate re-locatable code.
- **Execution time:** If the process can be moved during its execution from one memory segment to another, then binding must be delayed until run time.

7.1.1 Dynamic Loading

Better memory-space utilization can be done by dynamic loading. With dynamic loading, a routine is not loaded until it is called. All routines are kept on disk in a re-locatable load format. The main program is loaded into memory and is executed.

The advantage of dynamic loading is that an unused routine is never loaded.

7.1.2 Dynamic Linking

Most operating systems support only static linking, in which system language libraries are treated like any other object module and are combined by the loader into the binary program image. The concept of dynamic linking is similar to that of dynamic loading. Rather than loading being postponed until execution time, linking is postponed. This feature is usually used with system libraries, such as language subroutine libraries. With dynamic linking, a stub is included in the image for each library-routine reference. This stub is a small piece of code that indicates how to locate the appropriate memory-resident library routing.

The entire program and data of a process must be in physical memory for the process to execute. The size of a process is limited to the size of physical memory. So that a process can be larger than the amount of memory allocated to it, a technique called overlays is sometimes used. The idea of overlays is to keep in memory only those instructions and data that are needed at any given time. When other instructions are needed, they are loaded into space that was occupied previously by instructions that are no longer needed.

Example, consider a two-pass assembler. During pass 1, it constructs a symbol table; then, during pass 2, it generates machine-language code. We may be able to partition such an assembler into pass 1 code, pass 2 code, the symbol table 1, and common support routines used by both pass 1 and pass 2.

Let us consider

Pass 1	70K
Pass 2	80K
Symbol table	20K
Common routines	30K

To load everything at once, we would require 200K of memory. If only 150K is available, we cannot run our process. But pass 1 and pass 2 do not need to be in memory at the same time. We thus define two overlays: Overlay A is the symbol table, common routines, and pass 1, and overlay B is the symbol table, common routines, and pass 2.

We add an overlay driver (10K) and start with overlay A in memory. When we finish pass 1, we jump to the overlay driver, which reads overlay B into memory, overwriting overlay A, and then transfers control to pass 2. Overlay A needs only 120K, whereas overlay B needs 130K

As in dynamic loading, overlays do not require any special support from the operating system.

7.1.3 Logical versus Physical Address Space

An address generated by the CPU is commonly referred to as a logical address, whereas an address seen by the memory unit is commonly referred to as a physical address.

The compile-time and load-time address-binding schemes result in an environment where the logical and physical addresses are the same. The execution-time address-binding scheme results in an environment where the logical and physical addresses differ. In this case, we usually refer to the logical address as a virtual address. The set of all logical addresses generated by a program is referred to as a logical address space; the set of all physical addresses corresponding to these logical addresses is referred to as a physical address space.

The run-time mapping from virtual to physical addresses is done by the memory management unit (MMU), which is a hardware device.

The base register is called a relocation register. The value in the relocation register is added to every address generated by a user process at the time it is sent to memory. For example, if the base is at 13000, then an attempt by the user to address location 0 dynamically relocated to location 14,000; an access to location

347 is mapped to location 13347. The MS-DOS operating system running on the Intel 80x86 family of processors uses four relocation registers when loading and running processes.

The user program never sees the real physical addresses. The program can create a pointer to location 347 store it memory, manipulate it, compare it to other addresses all as the number 347.

The user program deals with logical addresses. The memory-mapping hardware converts logical addresses into physical addressed Logical addresses (in the range 0 to max) and physical addresses (in the range R + 0 to R + max for a base value R). The user generates only logical addresses.

The concept of a logical address space that is bound to a separate physical address space is central to proper memory management.

7.2 Swapping

A process, can be swapped temporarily out of memory to a backing store, and then brought back into memory for continued execution. Assume a multiprogramming environment with a round robin CPU-scheduling algorithm. When a quantum expires, the memory manager will start to swap out the process that just finished, and to swap in another process to the memory space that has been freed (Fig 7.2). When each process finishes its quantum, it will be swapped with another process.

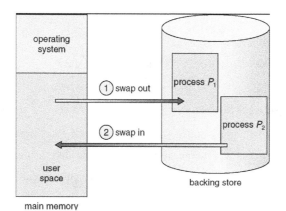

Fig 7.2 Swapping of two processes using a disk as a blocking store

A variant of this swapping policy is used for priority-based scheduling algorithms. If a higher-priority process arrives and wants service, the memory manager can swap out the lower-priority process so that it can load and execute the higher priority process. When the higher priority process finishes, the lower-priority process can be swapped back in and continued. This variant of swapping is sometimes called rollout, roll in. A process is swapped out will be swapped back into the same memory space that it occupies previously. If binding is done at assembly or load time, then the process cannot be moved to different location. If execution-time binding is being used, then it is possible to swap a process into a different memory space.

Swapping requires a backing store. The backing store is commonly a fast disk. It is large enough to accommodate copies of all memory images for all users. The system maintains a ready queue consisting of all processes whose memory images are on the backing store or in memory and are ready to run.

The context-switch time in such a swapping system is fairly high. Let us assume that the user process is of size 100K and the backing store is a standard hard disk with transfer rate of 1 megabyte per second. The actual transfer of the 100K process to or from memory takes

$$100K / 1000K \text{ per second} = 1/10 \text{ second}$$
$$= 100 \text{ milliseconds}$$

7.3 Contiguous Allocation

The main memory must accommodate both the operating system and the various user processes. The memory is usually divided into two partitions, one for the resident operating system, and one for the user processes.

To place the operating system in low memory. Thus, we shall discuss only me situation where the operating system resides in low memory (Figure 8.5). The development of the other situation is similar. Common Operating System is placed in low memory.

7.3.1 Single-Partition Allocation

If the operating system is residing in low memory, and the user processes are executing in high memory. And operating-system code and data are protected from changes by the user processes. We also need protect the user processes from one another. We can provide this 2 protection by using a relocation registers.

The relocation register contains the value of the smallest physical address; the limit register contains the range of logical addresses (for example, relocation = 100,040 and limit = 74,600). With relocation and limit registers, each logical address must be less than the limit register; the MMU maps the logical address dynamically by adding the value in the relocation register. This mapped address is sent to memory.

The relocation-register scheme provides an effective way to allow the operating system size to change dynamically.

7.3.2 Multiple-Partition Allocation

One of the simplest schemes for memory allocation is to divide memory into a number of fixed-sized partitions. Each partition may contain exactly one process. Thus, the degree of multiprogramming is bound by the number of partitions. When a partition is free, a process is selected from the input queue and is loaded into the free partition. When the process terminates, the partition becomes available for another process.

The operating system keeps a table indicating which parts of memory are available and which are occupied. Initially, all memory is available for user processes, and is considered as one large block, of available memory, a hole. When a process arrives and needs memory, we search for a hole large enough for this process.

For example, assume that we have 2560K of memory available and a resident operating system of 400K. This situation leaves 2160K for user processes. FCFS job scheduling, we can immediately allocate memory to processes P1, P2, P3. Holes size 260K that cannot be used by any of the remaining processes in the input queue. Using a round-robin CPU-scheduling with a quantum of 1 time unit, process will terminate at time 14, releasing its memory.

Memory allocation is done using Round-Robin Sequence as shown in fig. When a process arrives and needs memory, we search this set for a hole that is large enough for this process. If the hole is too large, it is split into two: One part is allocated to the arriving process; the other is returned to the set of holes. When a process terminates, it releases its block of memory, which is then placed back in the set of holes. If the new hole is adjacent to other holes, we merge these adjacent holes to form one larger hole.

This procedure is a particular instance of the general dynamic storage-allocation problem, which is how to satisfy a request of size n from a list of free holes. There are many solutions to this problem. The set of holes is searched to determine which hole is best to allocate, first-fit, best-fit, and worst-fit are the most common strategies used to select a free hole from the set of available holes.

- First-fit: Allocate the first hole that is big enough. Searching can start either at the beginning of the set of holes or where the previous first-fit search ended. We can stop searching as soon as we find a free hole that is large enough.
- Best-fit: Allocate the smallest hole that is big enough. We must search the entire list, unless the list is kept ordered by size. This strategy-produces the smallest leftover hole.
- Worst-fit: Allocate the largest hole. Again, we must search the entire list unless it is sorted by size. This strategy produces the largest leftover hole which may be more useful than the smaller leftover hole from a best-t approach.

7.3.3 External and Internal Fragmentation

As processes are loaded and removed from memory, the free memory space is broken into little pieces. External fragmentation exists when enough to the memory space exists to satisfy a request, but it is not contiguous; storage is fragmented into a large number of small holes.

Depending on the total amount of memory storage and the average process size, external fragmentation may be either a minor or a major problem.

Given N allocated blocks, another 0.5N blocks will be lost due to fragmentation. That is, one-third of memory may be unusable. This property is known as the 50- percent rule.

Internal fragmentation - memory that is internal to partition, but is not being used.

7.4 Paging

External fragmentation is avoided by using paging. In this physical memory is broken into blocks of the same size called pages. When a process is to be executed, its pages are loaded into any available memory frames. Every address generated by the CPU is divided into any two parts: a page number(p) and a page offset(d) (Fig 7.3). The page number is used as an index into a page table. The page table contains the base address of each page in physical memory. This base address is combined with the gage offset to define the physical memory address that is sent to the memory unit.

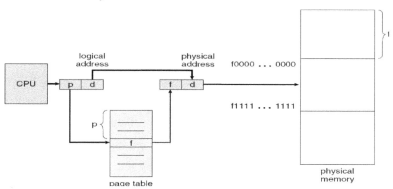

Fig 7.3 Paging Hardware

The page size like is defined by the hardware. The size of a page is typically a power of 2 varying between 512 bytes and 8192 bytes per page, depending on the computer architecture. The selection of a power of 2 as a page size makes the translation of a logical address into a page number and page offset. If the size of logical address space is 2^m, and a page size is 2^n addressing units (bytes or words), then the high-order m - n bits of a logical address designate the page number, and the n low-order bits designate the page offset. Thus, the logical address is as follows:

page number

page	offset
p	d
m − n	n

where p is an index into the page table and d is the displacement within the page.

Paging is a form of dynamic relocation. Every logical address is bound by the paging hardware to some physical address.

When we use a paging scheme, we have no external fragmentation: Any free frame can be allocated to a process that needs it.

If process size is independent of page size, we can have internal fragmentation to average one-half page per process.

When a process arrives in the system to be executed, its size, expressed in pages, is examined. Each page of the process needs one frame. Thus, if the process requires n pages, there must be at least n frames available in memory. If there are n frames available, they are allocated to this arriving process. The first page of the process is loaded into one of the allocated frames and the frame number is put in the page table for this process. The next page is loaded into another frame, and its frame number is put into the page table, and so on.

The user program views that memory as one single contiguous space, containing only this one program. But the user program is scattered throughout physical memory and logical addresses are translated into physical addresses.

The operating system is managing physical memory, it must be aware of the allocation details of physical memory: which frames are allocated, which frames are available, how many total frames there are, and so on. This information is generally kept in a data structure called a frame table. The frame table has one entry for each physical page frame, indicating whether the latter is free allocated and, if it is allocated, to which page of which process or processes.

The operating system maintains a copy of the page table for each process. Paging therefore increases the context-switch time.

7.5 Segmentation

A user program can be subdivided using segmentation, in which the program and its associated data are divided into a number of **segments.** It is not required that all segments of all programs be of the same length, although there is a maximum segment length. As with paging, a logical address using segmentation consists of two parts, in this case a segment number and an offset.

Because of the use of unequal-size segments, segmentation is similar to dynamic partitioning. In segmentation, a program may occupy more than one partition, and these partitions need not be contiguous. Segmentation eliminates internal fragmentation but, like dynamic partitioning, it suffers from external fragmentation. However, because a process is broken up into a number of smaller pieces, the external fragmentation should be less. Whereas paging is invisible to the programmer, segmentation usually visible and is provided as a convenience for organizing programs and data.

Another consequence of unequal-size segments is that there is no simple relationship between logical addresses and physical addresses. Segmentation scheme would make use of a segment table for each process and a list of free blocks of main memory. Each segment table entry would have to as in paging give the starting address in main memory of the corresponding segment. The entry should also provide the length of the segment, to assure that invalid addresses are not used. When a process enters the Running state, the address of its segment table is loaded into a special register used by the memory management hardware.

Consider an address of n + m bits, where the leftmost n bits are the segment number and the rightmost m bits are the offset. The following steps are needed for address translation:

- Extract the segment number as the leftmost n bits of the logical address.
- Use the segment number as an index into the process segment table to find the starting physical address of the segment.
- Compare the offset, expressed in the rightmost m bits, to the length of the segment. If the offset is greater than or equal to the length, the address is invalid.
- The desired physical address is the sum of the starting physical address of the segment plus the offset.

Segmentation and paging can be combined to have a good result.

7.6 Summary

Memory management algorithms for multi programmed operating systems range from the simple single user system approach to paged segmentation. The most important determinant of the method used in a particular system is the hardware provided, every memory address generated by the CPU must be checked for legality and possibly mapped to a physical address, the checking cannot be implemented in software. Hence, we are constrained by the hardware available.

The various memory management algorithms(continuous allocation, paging, segmentation, and combinations of paging and segmentation) differ in many aspects. In computing different memory management strategies, we use hardware support, performance, fragmentation, relocation, swapping, sharing and protection.

7.7 Model Question

Q.1   Differentiate internal and external fragmentation?

Q.2   Explain segmentation?

Q.3   What are hardware is required for paging?

Q.4   Write a note on virtual memory?

Q.5   Explain Page replacement algorithm in detail?

Q.6   compare demand paging and segmentation?

Q.7   Explain page replacement algorithm?

CHAPTER 8
VIRTUAL MEMORY

Unit Structure
8.0 Objectives

8.1 Virtual Memory

8.2 Demand Paging

8.3 Performance of demand paging

8.4 Virtual Memory Concepts

8.5 Page Replacement Algorithms

8.6 Allocation Algorithms

8.7 Summary

8.8 Model Question

8.0 Objective

- To describe the benefits of a virtual memory system.

- To explain the concepts of demand paging, page-replacement algorithms, and allocation of page frames.

- To discuss the principle of the working-set model.

8.1 Virtual Memory

- Virtual memory is a technique that allows the execution of process that may not be completely in memory. The main visible advantage of this scheme is that programs can be larger than physical memory.

- Virtual memory is the separation of user logical memory from physical memory this separation allows an extremely large virtual memory to be provided for programmers when only a smaller physical memory is available (Fig 8.1).
- Following are the situations, when entire program is not required to load fully.
1. User written error handling routines are used only when an error occurs in the data or computation.
2. Certain options and features of a program may be used rarely.
3. Many tables are assigned a fixed amount of address space even though only a small amount of the table is actually used.
- The ability to execute a program that is only partially in memory would counter many benefits.
1. Less number of I/O would be needed to load or swap each user program into memory.
2. A program would no longer be constrained by the amount of physical memory that is available.
3. Each user program could take less physical memory, more programs could be run the same time, with a corresponding increase in CPU utilization and throughput.

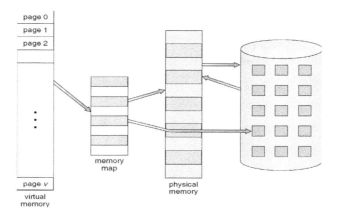

page 0
page 1
page 2
⋮
page *v*
virtual
memory

memory
map

physical
memory

Fig. 8.1 Diagram showing virtual memory that is larger than physical memory.

Virtual memory is commonly implemented by demand paging. It can also be implemented in a segmentation system. Demand segmentation can also be used to provide virtual memory.

8.2 Demand Paging

A demand paging is similar to a paging system with swapping(Fig 8.2). When we want to execute a process, we swap it into memory. Rather than swapping the entire process into memory.

When a process is to be swapped in, the pager guesses which pages will be used before the process is swapped out again Instead of swapping in a whole process, the pager brings only those necessary pages into memory. Thus, it avoids reading into memory pages that will not be used in anyway, decreasing the swap time and the amount of physical memory needed.

Hardware support is required to distinguish between those pages that are in memory and those pages that are on the disk using the valid-invalid bit scheme. Where valid and invalid pages can be checked checking the bit and marking a page will have no effect if the process never attempts to access the pages. While the process executes and accesses pages that are memory resident, execution proceeds normally.

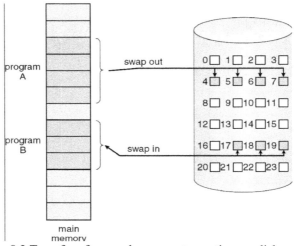

Fig. 8.2 Transfer of a paged memory to continuous disk space

Access to a page marked invalid causes a page-fault trap. This trap is the result of the operating system's failure to bring the desired page into memory. But page fault can be handled as following (Fig 8.3):

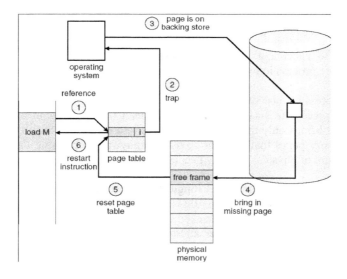

Fig. 8.3 Steps in handling a page fault

1. We check an internal table for this process to determine whether the reference was a valid or invalid memory access.
2. If the reference was invalid, we terminate the process. If .it was valid, but we have not yet brought in that page, we now page in the latter.
3. We find a free frame.

4. We schedule a disk operation to read the desired page into the newly allocated frame.

5. When the disk read is complete, we modify the internal table kept with the process and the page table to indicate that the page is now in memory.

6. We restart the instruction that was interrupted by the illegal address trap. The process can now access the page as though it had always been memory.

Therefore, the operating system reads the desired page into memory and restarts the process as though the page had always been in memory.

The page replacement is used to make the frame free if they are not in used. If no frame is free then other process is called in.

8.2.1 Advantages of Demand Paging:
1. Large virtual memory.
2. More efficient use of memory.
3. Unconstrained multiprogramming. There is no limit on degree of multiprogramming.

8.2.2 Disadvantages of Demand Paging:
1. Number of tables and amount of processor over head for handling page interrupts are greater than in the case of the simple paged management techniques.
2. due to the lack of an explicit constraints on a jobs address space size.

8.3 Page Replacement Algorithm

There are many different page replacement algorithms. We evaluate an algorithm by running it on a particular string of memory reference and computing the number of page faults. The string of memory references is called reference string. Reference strings are generated artificially or by tracing a given system and recording the address of each memory reference. The latter choice produces a large number of data.

1. For a given page size we need to consider only the page number, not the entire address.

2. if we have a reference to a page p, then any immediately following references to page p will never cause a page fault. Page p will be in memory after the first reference; the immediately following references will not fault.

Eg:- consider the address sequence
        0100, 0432, 0101, 0612, 0102, 0103, 0104, 0101, 0611, 0102, 0103,
        0104, 0101, 0610, 0102, 0103, 0104, 0104, 0101, 0609, 0102, 0105
    and reduce to 1, 4, 1, 6,1, 6, 1, 6, 1, 6, 1

To determine the number of page faults for a particular reference string and page replacement algorithm, we also need to know the number of page frames available. As the number of frames available increase, the number of page faults will decrease.

8.3.1 FIFO Algorithm

The simplest page-replacement algorithm is a FIFO algorithm. A FIFO replacement algorithm associates with each page the time when that page was brought into memory. When a page must be replaced, the oldest page is chosen. We can create a FIFO queue to hold all pages in memory.

The first three references (7, 0, 1) cause page faults, and are brought into these empty eg. 7, 0, 1, 2, 0, 3, 0, 4, 2, 3, 0, 3, 2, 1, 2, 0, 1 and consider 3 frames. This replacement means that the next reference to 0 will fault. Page 1 is then replaced by page 0.

8.3.2 Optimal Algorithm

An optimal page-replacement algorithm has the lowest page-fault rate of all algorithms. An optimal page-replacement algorithm exists, and has been called OPT or MIN. It is simply
                Replace the page that will not be used
                for the longest period of time.

Now consider the same string with 3 empty frames.

The reference to page 2 replaces page 7, because 7 will not be used until reference 18, whereas page 0 will be used at 5, and page 1 at 14. The reference to page 3 replaces page 1, as page 1 will be the last of the three pages in memory to be referenced again. Optimal replacement is much better than a FIFO.

The optimal page-replacement algorithm is difficult to implement, because it requires future knowledge of the reference string.

8.3.3 LRU Algorithm

The FIFO algorithm uses the time when a page was brought into memory; the OPT algorithm uses the time when a page is to be used. In LRU replace the page that has not been used for the longest period of time.

LRU replacement associates with each page the time of that page's last use. When a page must be replaced, LRU chooses that page that has not been used for the longest period of time.

Let S^R be the reverse of a reference string S, then the page-fault rate for the OPT algorithm on S is the same as the page-fault rate for the OPT algorithm on S^R.

8.3.4 LRU Approximation Algorithms

Some systems provide no hardware support, and other page-replacement algorithm. Many systems provide some help, however, in the form of a reference bit. The reference bit for a page is set, by the hardware, whenever that page is referenced. Reference bits are associated with each entry in the page table Initially, all bits are cleared (to 0) by the operating system. As a user process executes, the bit associated with each page referenced is set (to 1) by the hardware.

8.3.4.1 Additional-Reference-Bits Algorithm

The operating system shifts the reference bit for each page into the high-order or of its 8-bit byte, shifting the other bits right 1 bit, discarding the low-order bit.

These 8-bit shift registers contain the history of page use for the last eight time periods. If the shift register contains 00000000, then the page has not been used for eight time periods; a page that is used at least once each period would have a shift register value of 11111111.

8.3.4.2 Second-Chance Algorithm

The basic algorithm of second-chance replacement is a FIFO replacement algorithm. When a page gets a second chance, its reference bit is cleared and its arrival e is reset to the current time.

8.3.4.3 Enhanced Second-Chance Algorithm

The second-chance algorithm described above can be enhanced by considering troth the reference bit and the modify bit as an ordered pair.

1. (0,0) neither recently used nor modified best page to replace.
2. (0,1) not recently used but modified not quite as good, because the page will need to be written out before replacement.
3. (1,0) recently used but clean probably will be used again soon.
4. (1,1) recently used and modified probably will be used again, and write out will be needed before replacing it

8.4 Counting Algorithms

There are many other algorithms that can be used for page replacement.

• **LFU Algorithm:** The least frequently used (LFU) page-replacement algorithm requires that the page with the smallest count be replaced. This algorithm suffers from the situation in which a page is used heavily during the initial phase of a process, but then is never used again.

• **MFU Algorithm:** The most frequently used (MFU) page-replacement algorithm is based on the argument that the page with the smallest count was probably just brought in and has yet to be used.

8.5 Page Buffering Algorithm

When a page fault occurs, a victim frame is chosen as before. However, the desired page is read into a free frame from the pool before the victim is written out.

This procedure allows the process to restart as soon as possible, without waiting for the victim page to be written out. When the victim is later written out, its frame is added to the free-frame pool.

When the FIFO replacement algorithm mistakenly replaces a page mistakenly replaces a page that is still in active use, that page is quickly retrieved from the free-frame buffer, and no I/O is necessary. The free-frame buffer provides protection against the relatively poor, but simple, FIFO replacement algorithm.

8.6 Summary

It is desirable to be able to execute a process whose logical address space larger than the available physical address space. Virtual memory is a technique that enables us to map a logical address space onto a smaller physical memory. Virtual memory allows us to run extremely large processes and to raise the degree of multiprogramming, increasing CPU utilization. Virtual memory also enables us to use an efficient type of process creation known as copy-on-write, where in parent and child processes share actual pages of memory.

Virtual memory is commonly implemented by demand paging. pure demand paging never brings in a page until that page is referenced. The first reference causes page fault to the operating system. If total memory requirements exceed the capacity of physical memory, then it may be necessary to replace pages from memory to free frames for new pages. Various page replacement algorithm are used.

In addition to a page replacement algorithm, a frame allocation policy is needed. Allocation can be fixed, suggesting local page replacement, or dynamic, suggesting global replacement.

8.7 Model Question

Q.1   Define and explain Virtual Memory?

Q.2   Explain advantages and disadvantages Demand Paging

Q.3   Define and explain Performance of demand paging?

Q.4   Describe Page Replacement Algorithms?

Q.5   Explain various Allocation Algorithms?

CHAPTER 9
I/O HARDWARE

Unit Structure

9.0   Objective

- Explore the structure of an operating system's I/O subsystem.

- Discuss the principles of I/O hardware and its complexity.

9.1 I/O Hardware

- Computers operate a great many kinds of devices. General types include storage devices (disks, tapes), transmission devices (network cards, modems), and human-interface devices (screen, keyboard, mouse).
- A device communicates with a computer system by sending signals over a cable or even through the air. The device communicates with the machine

via a connection point termed a port (for example, a serial port). If one or more devices use a common set of wires, the connection is called a bus.

- When device A has a cable that plugs into device B, and device B has a cable that plugs into device C, and device C plugs into a port on the computer, this arrangement is called a daisy chain. It usually operates as a bus.
- A controller is a collection of electronics that can operate a port, a bus, or a device. A serial-port controller is an example of a simple device controller. It is a single chip in the computer that controls the signals on the wires of a serial port.
- The SCSI bus controller is often implemented as a separate circuit board (a host adapter) that plugs into the computer. It typically contains a processor, microcode, and some private memory to enable it to process the SCSI protocol messages. Some devices have their own built-in controllers.
- An I/O port typically consists of four registers, called the status, control, data-in, and data-out registers. The status register contains bits that can be read by the host. These bits indicate states such as whether the current command has completed, whether a byte is available to be read from the data-in register, and whether there has been a device error. The control register can be written by the host to start a command or to change the mode of a device. For instance, a certain bit in the control register of a serial port chooses between full-duplex and half-duplex communication, another enables parity checking, a third bit sets the word length to 7 or 8 bits, and other bits select one of the speeds supported by the serial port.
- The data-in register is read by the host to get input, and the data out register is written by the host to send output. The data registers are typically 1 to 4 bytes. Some controllers have FIFO chips that can hold several bytes of input or output data to expand the capacity of the controller beyond the size of the data register. A FIFO chip can hold a small burst of data until the device or host is able to receive those data.

9.2 POLLING

- Incomplete protocol for interaction between the host and a controller can be intricate, but the basic handshaking notion is simple. The controller indicates its state through the busy bit in the status register. (Recall that to set a bit means to write a 1 into the bit, and to clear a bit means to write a 0 into it.)
- The controller sets the busy bit when it is busy working, and clears the busy bit when it is ready to accept the next command. The host signals its wishes via the command-ready bit in the command register. The host sets the

command-ready bit when a command is available for the controller to execute.

- For this example, the host writes output through a port, coordinating with the controller by handshaking as follows.

1. The host repeatedly reads the busy bit until that bit becomes clear.
2. The host sets the write bit in the command register and writes a byte into the data-out register.
3. The host sets the command-ready bit.
4. When the controller notices that the command-ready bit is set, it sets the Busy.
5. The controller reads the command register and sees the write command.
6. It reads the data-out register to get the byte, and does the I/O to the device.
7. The controller clears the command-ready bit, clears the error bit in the status register to indicate that the device I/O succeeded, and clears the busy bit to indicate that it is finished.

- The host is busy-waiting or polling: It is in a loop, reading the status register over and over until the busy bit becomes clear. If the controller and device are fast, this method is a reasonable one. But if the wait may be long, the host should probably switch to another task

9.3 I/O Devices

- Categories of I/O Devices

1. Human readable

2. machine readable

3. Communication

1. Human Readable is suitable for communicating with the computer user. Examples are printers, video display terminals, keyboard etc.

2. Machine Readable is suitable for communicating with electronic equipment. Examples are disk and tape drives, sensors, controllers and actuators.

3. Communication is suitable for communicating with remote devices. Examples are digital line drivers and modems.

- Differences between I/O Devices

1. Data rate : there may be differences of several orders of magnitude between the data transfer rates.
2. Application: Different devices have different use in the system.
3. Complexity of Control: A disk is much more complex whereas printer requires simple control interface.
4. Unit of transfer: Data may be transferred as a stream of bytes or characters or in larger blocks.
5. Data representation: Different data encoding schemes are used for different devices.
6. Error Conditions: The nature of errors differs widely from one device to another.

9.4 Direct Memory Access

- A special control unit may be provided to allow transfer of a block of data directly between an external device and the main memory, without continuous intervention by the processor. This approach is called Direct Memory Access(DMA).
- DMA can be used with either polling or interrupt software. DMA is particularly useful on devices like disks, where many bytes of information can be transferred in single I/O operations. When used in conjunction with an interrupt, the CPU is notified only after the entire block of data has been

transferred. For each byte or word transferred, it must provide the memory address and all the bus signals that control the data transfer.

- Interaction with a device controller is managed through a device driver.
- Device drivers are part of the operating system, but not necessarily part of the OS kernel. The operating system provides a simplified view of the device to user applications (e.g., character devices vs. block devices in UNIX). In some operating systems (e.g., Linux), devices are also accessible through the /dev file system.
- In some cases, the operating system buffers data that are transferred between a device and a user space program (disk cache, network buffer). This usually increases performance, but not always.

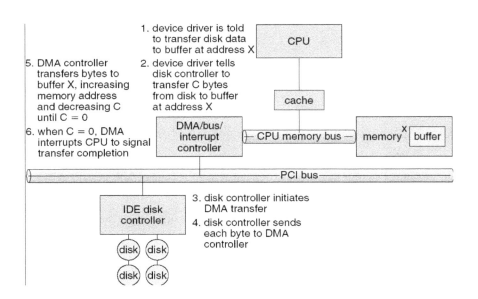

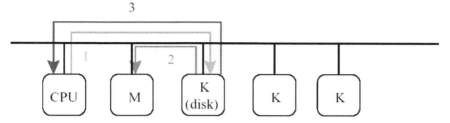

1. CPU issues DMA request to controller
2. controller directs data transfer
3. controller interrupts CPU

9.5 Device Controllers

A computer system contains a multitude of I/O devices and their respective controllers:

- network card
- graphics adapter
- disk controller
- DVD-ROM controller
- serial port
- USB
- sound card

9.6 Summary

The basic hardware elements involved in I/O buses, device controllers, and the device themselves. The work of moving data between devices and main memory is performed by the CPU as programmed I/O or is offloaded to a DMA controller. The kernel module that controls a device driver.

The system call interface provided to applications is designed to handle several basic categories of hardware, including block devices, character devices, memory mapped files, network sockets, and programmed interval timers. The system calls usually block the processes that issue them, but non blocking and asynchronous calls are used by the kernel itself and by applications that must not sleep while waiting for an I/O operation to complete.

The kernel's I/O subsystem provides numerous services. Among these are I/O scheduling, buffering, caching. Spooling, device reservation, and error handling.

9.7 Model Question

Q.1   Define and Explain Direct Memory Access?
Q.2   Explain device controllers?
Q.3   Explain concept of I/O Hardware?
Q.4   Explain concept of Polling?
Q.5   Explain I/O devices?

CHAPTER 10
I/O SOFTWARE

Unit Structure
10.0 Objectives

10.1 Principle of I/O Software

      10.1.1 Interrupts

      10.2.2 Application I/O Interfaced

      10.1.3 Clocks and Timers

      10.1.4 Blocking and Non-blocking I/O

10.2 Kernel I/O Subsystem

      10.2.1 Scheduling

      10.2.2 Buffering

      10.2.3 Caching

10.0 Objective

- Explore the structure of an operating system's I/O subsystem.
- Discuss the principles of I/O software.
- Provide details of the performance aspects of I/O software.

10.1 PRINCIPLES OF I/O SOFTWARE

10.1.1 Interrupts

- The CPU hardware has a wire called the interrupt request line that the CPU senses after executing every instruction. When the CPU detects that a controller has asserted a signal on the interrupt request line, the CPU saves a small amount of state, such as the current value of the instruction pointer, and jumps to the interrupt-handler routine at a fixed address in memory.

- The interrupt handler determines the cause of the interrupt, performs the necessary processing, and executes a return from interrupt instruction to return the CPU to the execution state prior to the interrupt. We say that the device controller raises an interrupt by asserting a signal on the interrupt request line, the CPU catches the interrupt and dispatches to the interrupt handler, and the handler clears the interrupt by servicing the device. Figure 12.3 summarizes the interrupt-driven I/O cycle.

- This basic interrupt mechanism enables the CPU to respond to an asynchronous event, such as a device controller becoming ready for service. In a modern operating system, we need more sophisticated interrupt-handling features.

- First, we need the ability to defer interrupt handling during critical processing. Second, we need an efficient way to dispatch to the proper interrupt handler for a device, without first polling all the devices to see which one raised the interrupt. Third, we need multilevel interrupts, so that the operating system can distinguish between high- and low-priority interrupts, and can respond with the appropriate degree of urgency.

- In modern computer hardware, these three features are provided by the CPU and by the interrupt-controller hardware.

- CPUs have two interrupt request lines. One is the non-maskable interrupt, which is reserved for events such as unrecoverable memory errors. The second interrupt line is maskable. It can be turned off by the CPU before the execution of critical instruction sequences that must not be interrupted. The maskable interrupt is used by device controllers to request service.

- This address is an offset in a table called the interrupt vector. This vector contains the memory addresses of .specialized interrupt handlers. The purpose of a vectored interrupt mechanism is to reduce the need for a single interrupt handler to search all possible sources of interrupts to determine which one needs service.

- The interrupt mechanism also implements a system of interrupt priority levels. This mechanism enables the CPU to defer the handling of low-priority interrupts without masking off all interrupts, and makes it possible for a high-priority interrupt to preempt the execution of a low-priority interrupt.

- The interrupt mechanism is also used to handle a wide variety of exceptions, such as dividing by zero, accessing a protected or nonexistent memory address, or attempting to execute a privileged instruction from user mode.
- A system call is a function that is called by an application to invoke a kernel service. The system call checks the arguments given by the application, builds a data structure to convey the arguments to the kernel, and then executes a special instruction called a software interrupt, or a trap.
- Interrupts can also be used to manage the flow of control within the kernel. If the disks are to be used efficiently, we need to start the next I/O as soon as the previous one completes. Consequently, the kernel code that completes a disk read is implemented by a pair of interrupt handlers. The high-priority handler records the I/O status, clears the device interrupt, starts the next pending I/O, and raises a low-priority interrupt to complete the work. The corresponding handler completes the user level I/O by copying data from kernel buffers to the application space and then by calling the scheduler to place the application on the ready queue.

10.2.2 Application I/O Interfaced

- Structuring techniques and interfaces for the operating system enable I/O devices to be treated in a standard, uniform way. For instance, how an application can open a file on a disk without knowing what kind of disk it is, and how new disks and other devices can be added to a computer without the operating system being disrupted.

- The actual differences are encapsulated in ken modules called device drivers mat internally are custom tailored to each device but that export one of the standard interfaces.
- The purpose of the device-driver layer is to hide the differences among device controllers from the I/O subsystem of the kernel, much as the I/O system calls.

Character-stream or block. A character-stream device transfers bytes one by one, whereas a block device transfers a block of bytes as a unit.

Sequential or random-access. A sequential device transfers data in a fixed order that is determined by the device, whereas the user of a random-access device can instruct the device to seek to any of the available data storage locations.

Synchronous or asynchronous. A synchronous device is one that performs data transfers with predictable response times. An asynchronous device exhibits irregular or unpredictable response times.

Sharable or dedicated. A sharable device can be used concurrently by several processes or threads; a dedicated device cannot.

Speed of operation. Device speeds range from a few bytes per second to a few gigabytes per second.

Read-write, read only, or write only. Some devices perform both input and output, but others support only one data direction. For the purpose of application access, many of these differences are hidden by the operating system, and the devices are grouped into a few conventional types.

- Operating systems also provide special system calls to access a few additional devices, such as a time-of-day clock and a timer. The performance and addressing characteristics of network I/O differ significantly from those of disk I/O, most operating systems provide a network I/O interface that is different from the **read-write-seek** interface used for disks.

10.1.3 Clocks and Timers

- Most computers have hardware clocks and timers that provide three basic functions:
1. Give the current time
2. Give the elapsed time
3. Set a timer to trigger operation X at time T
- These functions are used heavily by the operating system, and also by time sensitive applications. The hardware to measure elapsed time and to trigger operations is called a programmable interval timer.

10.1.4 Blocking and Non-blocking I/O

- One remaining aspect of the system-call interface relates to the choice between blocking I/O and non-blocking (asynchronous) I/O. When an application calls a blocking system call, the execution of the application is suspended. The application is moved from the operating system's run queue to a wait queue.
- After the system call completes, the application is moved back to the run queue, where it is eligible to resume execution, at which time it will receive the values returned by the system call.
- Some user-level processes need non-blocking I/O.

10.2 Kernel I/O Subsystem

- Kernels provide many services related to I/O. The services that we describe are I/O scheduling, buffering caching, spooling, device reservation, and error handling.

10.2.1 Scheduling

- To schedule a set of I/O requests means to determine a good order in which to execute them. The order in which applications issue system calls rarely is the best choice. Scheduling can improve overall system performance, can share device access fairly among processes, and can reduce the average waiting time for I/O to complete. Operating-system developers implement scheduling by maintaining a queue of requests for each device. When an application issues a blocking I/O system call, the request is placed on the queue for that device.

- The I/O scheduler rearranges the order of the queue to improve the overall system efficiency and the average response time experienced by applications.

10.2.2 Buffering

- A buffer is a memory area that stores data while they are transferred between two devices or between a device arid an application. Buffering is done for three reasons.

- One reason is to cope with a speed mismatch between the producer and consumer of a data stream.

- Second buffer while the first buffer is written to disk. A second use of buffering is to adapt between devices that have different data transfer sizes.

- A third use of buffering is to support copy semantics for application I/O.

10.2.3 Caching

- A cache is region of fast memory that holds copies of data. Access to the cached copy is more efficient than access to the original.
- Caching and buffering are two distinct functions, but sometimes a region of memory can be used for both purposes.

10.2.3 Spooling and Device Reservation

- A spool is a buffer that holds output for a device, such as a printer, that cannot accept interleaved data streams. The spooling system copies the queued spool files to the printer one at a time.
- In some operating systems, spooling is managed by a system daemon process. In other operating systems, it is handled by an in kernel thread.

10.2.4 Error Handling

An operating system that uses protected memory can guard against many kinds of hardware and application errors.

10.3 Device drivers

- In computing, a device driver or software driver is a computer program allowing higher-level computer programs to interact with a hardware device.
- A driver typically communicates with the device through the computer bus or communications subsystem to which the hardware connects. When a calling program invokes a routine in the driver, the driver issues commands to the device.

- Once the device sends data back to the driver, the driver may invoke routines in the original calling program. Drivers are hardware-dependent and operating-system-specific.
- They usually provide the interrupt handling required for any necessary asynchronous time-dependent hardware interface.

10.4 Summary

The system call interface provided to applications is designed to handle several basic categories of hardware, including block devices, character devices, memory mapped files, network sockets, and programmed interval timers. The system calls usually block the processes that issue them, but non blocking and asynchronous calls are used by the kernel itself and by applications that must not sleep while waiting for an I/O operation to complete.

The kernel's I/O subsystem provides numerous services. Among these are I/O scheduling, buffering, caching. Spooling, device reservation, and error handling. I/O system calls are costly in terms of CPU consumption because of the many layers of software between a physical device and an application.

10.5 Model Question

Q.1   Explain application of I/O interface?

Q.2   Describe blocking and non blocking I/O?

Q.3   Explain following concepts

a) Clock and Timers

b) Device Drivers

Q.4   Write a short notes on

a) Scheduling

b) Buffering

c) Error Handling

Q.5   Explain spooling mechanism?

Q.6   Explain Caching in details?

CHAPTER 11
SECONDARY STORADE MANAGEMENT

Unit Structure
11.0 Objectives

11.1 Disk Structure

11.2 Disk Scheduling

11.3 Disk Management

11.4 Swap Space Management

11.5 Disk Reliability

11.6 Stable Storage Implementation

11.7 Summary

11.8 Model Question

11.0 Objective

- Describe the physical structure of secondary and tertiary storage devices and the resulting effects on the uses of the devices.

- Explain the performance characteristics of mass-storage devices.

- Discuss operating-system services provided for mass storage.

11.1 Disk Structure

- Disk provide bulk of secondary storage of computer system. The disk can be considered the one I/O device that is common to each and every computer. Disks come in many size and speeds, and information may be stored optically or magnetically. Magnetic tape was used as an early secondary storage medium, but the access time is much slower than for disks. For backup, tapes are currently used.

- Modern disk drives are addressed as large one dimensional arrays of logical blocks, where the logical block is the smallest unit of transfer. The actual details of disk I/O operation depends on the computer system, the operating system and the nature of the I/O channel and disk controller hardware.

- The basic unit of information storage is a sector. The sectors are stored on a flat, circular, media disk. This media spins close to one or more read/write heads. The heads can move from the inner portion of the disk to the outer portion.

- When the disk drive is operating, the disk is rotating at constant speed. To read or write, the head must be positioned at the desired track and at the beginning of the desired sector on that track. Track selection involves moving the head in a movable head system or electronically selecting one head on a fixed head system. These characteristics are common to floppy disks, hard disks, CD-ROM and DVD.

11.2 Disk Performance Parameters

- When the disk drive is operating, the disk is rotating at constant speed. To read or write, the head must be positioned at the desired track and at the beginning of the desired sector on that track.
- Track selection involves moving the head in a movable-head system or electronically selecting one head on a fixed-head system. On a movable-head system, the time it takes to position the head at the track is known as **seek time.**
- When once the track is selected, the disk controller waits until the appropriate sector rotates to line up with the head. The time it takes for the beginning of the sector to reach the head is known as **rotational delay,** or rotational latency. The sum of the seek time, if any, and the rotational delay equals the **access time,** which is the time it takes to get into position to read or write.
- Once the head is in position, the read or write operation is then performed as the sector moves under the head; this is the data transfer portion of the operation; the time required for the transfer is the **transfer time.**
- **Seek Time** Seek time is the time required to move the disk arm to the required track. It turns out that this is a difficult quantity to pin down. The seek time consists of two key components: the initial startup time and the time taken to traverse the tracks that have to be crossed once the access arm is up to speed.

    $$T_s = m \times n + s$$

- **Rotational Delay** Disks, other than floppy disks, rotate at speeds ranging from 3600 rpm up to, as of this writing, 15,000 rpm; at this latter speed, there is one revolution per 4 ms. Thus, on the average, the rotational delay will be 2 ms. Floppy disks typically rotate at between 300 and 600 rpm. Thus the average delay will be between 100 and 50 ms.

- **Transfer Time** The transfer time to or from the disk depends on the rotation speed of the disk in the following fashion:

$$T = b/rN$$

where

T = transfer time

b = number of bytes to be transferred

N = number of bytes on a track

r = rotation speed, in revolutions per second

Thus the total average access time can be expressed as

$$Ta = Ts +$$

where Ts is the average seek time.

11.3 Disk Scheduling

- The amount of head needed to satisfy a series of I/O request can affect the performance. If desired disk drive and controller are available, the request can be serviced immediately. If a device or controller is busy, any new requests for service will be placed on the queue of pending requests for that drive. When one request is completed, the operating system chooses which pending request to service next.
- Different types of scheduling algorithms are as follows.
    1. First Come, First Served scheduling algorithm(FCFS).
    2. Shortest Seek Time First (SSTF) algorithm
    3. SCAN algorithm
    4. Circular SCAN (C-SCAN) algorithm

5. Look Scheduling Algorithm

11.3.1 First Come, First Served scheduling algorithm(FCFS).

- The simplest form of scheduling is first-in-first-out (FIFO) scheduling, which processes items from the queue in sequential order. This strategy has the advantage of being fair, because every request is honored and the requests are honored in the order received. With FIFO, if there are only a few processes that require access and if many of the requests are to clustered file sectors, then we can hope for good performance.

- **Priority** With a system based on priority (PRI), the control of the scheduling is outside the control of disk management software.

- **Last In First Out** ln transaction processing systems, giving the device to the most recent user should result. In little or no arm movement for moving through a sequential file. Taking advantage of this locality improves throughput and reduces queue length.

11.3.2 Shortest Seek Time First (SSTF) algorithm

- The SSTF policy is to select the disk I/O request the requires the least movement of the disk arm from its current position. **Scan** With the exception of FIFO, all of the policies described so far can leave some request unfulfilled until the entire queue is emptied. That is, there may always be new requests arriving that will be chosen before an existing request.

- The choice should provide better performance than FCFS algorithm.

- Under heavy load, SSTF can prevent distant request from ever being serviced. This phenomenon is known as starvation. SSTF scheduling is essentially a from of shortest job first scheduling. SSTF scheduling algorithm are not very popular because of two reasons.

1. Starvation possibly exists.
2. it increases higher overheads.

11.3.3 SCAN scheduling algorithm

- The scan algorithm has the head start at track 0 and move towards the highest numbered track, servicing all requests for a track as it passes the track. The service direction is then reserved and the scan proceeds in the opposite direction, again picking up all requests in order.
- SCAN algorithm is guaranteed to service every request in one complete pass through the disk. SCAN algorithm behaves almost identically with the SSTF algorithm. The SCAN algorithm is sometimes called elevator algorithm.

11.3.4 C SCAN Scheduling Algorithm

- The C-SCAN policy restricts scanning to one direction only. Thus, when the last track has been visited in one direction, the arm is returned to the opposite end of the disk and the scan begins again.
- This reduces the maximum delay experienced by new requests.

11.3.5 LOOK Scheduling Algorithm

- Start the head moving in one direction. Satisfy the request for the closest track in that direction when there is no more request in the direction, the head is traveling, reverse direction and repeat. This algorithm is similar to innermost and outermost track on each circuit.

11.4 Disk Management

Operating system is responsible for disk management. Following are some activities discussed.

11.4.1 Disk Formatting

Disk formatting is of two types.

a) Physical formatting or low level formatting.

b) Logical Formatting

Physical Formatting

- Disk must be formatted before storing data.
- Disk must be divided into sectors that the disk controllers can read/write.
- Low level formatting files the disk with a special data structure for each sector.
- Data structure consists of three fields: header, data area and trailer.
- Header and trailer contain information used by the disk controller.
- Sector number and Error Correcting Codes (ECC) contained in the header and trailer.
- For writing data to the sector – ECC is updated.
- For reading data from the sector – ECC is recalculated.
- Low level formatting is done at factory.

Logical Formatting

- After disk is partitioned, logical formatting used.
- Operating system stores the initial file system data structures onto the disk.

11.4.2 Boot Block

- When a computer system is powered up or rebooted, a program in read only memory executes.

- Diagnostic check is done first.
- Stage 0 boot program is executed.
- Boot program reads the first sector from the boot device and contains a stage-1 boot program.
- May be boot sector will not contain a boot program.
- PC booting from hard disk, the boot sector also contains a partition table.
- The code in the boot ROM instructs the disk controller to read the boot blocks into memory and then starts executing that code.
- Full boot strap program is more sophisticated than the bootstrap loader in the boot ROM.

11.5 Swap Space Management

Swap space management is low level task of the operating system. The main goal for the design and implementation of swap space is to provide the best throughput for the virtual memory system.

11.5.1 Swap-Space Use

The operating system needs to release sufficient main memory to bring in a process that is ready to execute. Operating system uses this swap space in various way. Paging systems may simply store pages that have been pushed out of main memory. Unix operating system allows the use of multiple swap space are usually put on separate disks, so the load placed on the I/O system by paging and swapping can be spread over the systems I/O devices.

11.5.2 Swap Space Location

- Swap space can reside in two places:
    1. Separate disk partition

2. Normal file System

- If the swap space is simply a large file within the file system, normal file system routines can be used to create it, name it and allocate its space. This is easy to implement but also inefficient. External fragmentation can greatly increase swapping times. Catching is used to improve the system performance. Block of information is cached in the physical memory, and by using special tools to allocate physically continuous blocks for the swap file.

- Swap space can be created in a separate disk partition. No file system or directory structure is placed on this space. A separate swap space storage manager is used to allocate and deallocate the blocks. This manager uses algorithms optimized for speed. Internal fragmentation may increase. Some operating systems are flexible and can swap both in raw partitions and in file system space.

11.6 Stable Storage Implementation

- The write ahead log, which required the availability of stable storage.
- By definition, information residing in stable storage is never lost.
- To implement such storage, we need to replicate the required information on multiple storage devices (usually disks) with independent failure modes.
- We also need to coordinate the writing of updates in a way that guarantees that a failure during an update will not leave all the copies in a damaged state and that, when we are recovering from failure, we can force all copies to a consistent and correct value, even if another failure occurs during the recovery.

11.6 Disk Reliability

- Good performance means high speed, another important aspect of performance is reliability.
- A fixed disk drive is likely to be more reliable than a removable disk or tape drive.
- An optical cartridge is likely to be more reliable than a magnetic disk or tape.
- A head crash in a fixed hard disk generally destroys the data, whereas the failure of a tape drive or optical disk drive often leaves the data cartridge unharmed.

11.7 Summary

Disk drives are the major secondary storage I/O devices on most computers. Most secondary devices are either magnetic disks or magnetic tapes. Modern disk drives are structured as large one dimensional arrays of logical disk blocks. Disk scheduling algorithms can improve the effective bandwidth, the average response time, and the variance response time. Algorithms such as SSTF, SCAN, C-SCAN. LOOK, and CLOOK are designed to make such improvements through strategies for disk queue ordering.

Performance can be harmed by external fragmentation. The operating system manages block. First, a disk must be low level formatted to create the sectors on the raw hardware, new disks usually come preformatted. Then, disk is partitioned, file systems are created, and boot blocks are allocated to store the system bootstrap program. Finally when a block is corrupted, the system must have a way to lock out that block or to replace it logically with a space.

Because of efficient swap space is a key to good performance, systems usually bypass the file system and use raw disk access for paging I/O. Some systems dedicate a raw disk partition to swap space, and others use a file within the file system instead.

11.8 Model Question

Q.1   Explain disk structure?

Q.2   Explain following scheduling algorithms:

1. First Come, First Served scheduling algorithm(FCFS).

2. Shortest Seek Time First (SSTF) algorithm

3. SCAN algorithm

4. Circular SCAN (C-SCAN) algorithm

5. Look Scheduling Algorithm

Q.3   Explain swap space management?

Q. 4   Explain Disk management and types?
Q.5   Describe disk reliability?

CHAPTER 12
FILE SYSTEMS

Unit Structure
12.0 Objectives

12.1 File Concept

12.2 File Support

12.3 Access Methods

12.4 Directory Systems

12.5 File Protection

12.6 Free Space Management

12.7 Summary

12.8 Model Question

12.0 Objective
- To explain the function of file systems.
- To describe the interfaces to the file systems.
- To discuss file system design tradeoffs, including access methods, file sharing, file locking, and directory structure.
- To explore file system protection.

12.1 File Concept
❖ A file is a collection of similar records. The file is treated as a single entity by users and applications and may be referred by name. Files have unique file names and may be created and deleted. Restrictions on access control usually apply at the file level.

❖ A file is a container for a collection of information. The file manager provides a protection mechanism to allow users administrator how processes executing on behalf of different users can access the information in a file. File protection is a fundamental property of files because it allows different people to store their information on a shared computer.

❖ File represents programs and data. Data files may be numeric, alphabetic, binary or alpha numeric. Files may be free form, such as text files. In general, file is sequence of bits, bytes, lines or records.

❖ A file has a certain defined structure according to its type.

1 Text File
2 Source File
3 Executable File
4 Object File

File Structure

Four terms are use for files

• Field

• Record

• Database

A field is the basic element of data. An individual field contains a single value. A record is a collection of related fields that can be treated as a unit by some application program.

A file is a collection of similar records. The file is treated as a singly entity by users and applications and may be referenced by name. Files have file names and maybe created and deleted. Access control restrictions usually apply at the file level.

A database is a collection of related data. Database is designed for use by a number of different applications. A database may contain all of the information related to an organization or project, such as a business or a scientific study. The database itself consists of one or more types of files. Usually, there is a separate database management system that is independent of the operating system.

File Attributes
- File attributes vary from one operating system to another. The common attributes are,

    - **Name** – only information kept in human-readable form.

    - **Identifier** – unique tag (number) identifies file within file system

    - **Type** – needed for systems that support different types

    - **Location** – pointer to file location on device

    - **Size** – current file size

    - **Protection** – controls who can do reading, writing, executing

- **Time, date, and user identification** – data for protection, security, and usage monitoring

- Information about files are kept in the directory structure, which is maintained on the disk

File Operations

Any file system provides not only a means to store data organized as files, but a collection of functions that can be performed on files. Typical operations include the following:

Create: A new file is defined and positioned within the structure of files.

Delete: A file is removed from the file structure and destroyed.

Open: An existing file is declared to be "opened" by a process, allowing the process to perform functions on the file.

Close: The file is closed with respect to a process, so that the process no longer may perform functions on the file, until the process opens the file again.

Read: A process reads all or a portion of the data in a file.

Write: A process updates a file, either by adding new data that expands the size of the file or by changing the values of existing data items in the file.

File Types – Name, Extension

- A common technique for implementing file types is to include the type as part of the file name. The name is split into two parts : a name and an extension. Following table gives the file type with usual extension and function.

File Type	Usual Extension	Function
Executable	exe, com, bin	Read to run machine language program.
Object	obj, o	Compiled, machine language, not linked
Source Code	c, cc, java, pas asm, a	Source code in various language
Text	txt, doc	Textual data, documents

File Management Systems:

A file management system is that set of system software that provides services to users and applications in the use of files. following objectives for a file management system:

• To meet the data management needs and requirements of the user which include storage of data and the ability to perform the aforementioned operations.

• To guarantee, to the extent possible, that the data in the file are valid.

• To optimize performance, both from the system point of view in terms of overall throughput.

• To provide I/O support for a variety of storage device types.

• To minimize or eliminate the potential for lost or destroyed data.

• To provide a standardized set of I/O interface routines to use processes.

TO provide I/O support for multiple users, in the case of multiple-user systems **File System Architecture.** At the lowest level, **device drivers** communicate directly with peripheral devices or their controllers or channels. A device driver is responsible for starting I/O operations on a device and processing the completion of an I/O request. For file operations, the typical devices controlled are disk and tape drives. Device drivers are usually considered to be part of the operating system.

The I/O control, consists of device drivers and interrupt handlers to transfer information between the memory and the disk system. A device driver can be thought of as a translator.

The basic file system needs only to issue generic commands to the appropriate device driver to read and write physical blocks on the disk.

The file-organization module knows about files and their logical blocks, as well as physical blocks. By knowing the type of file allocation used and the location of the file, the file-organization module can translate logical block addresses to physical block addresses for the basic file system to transfer. Each file's logical blocks are numbered from 0 (or 1) through N, whereas the physical blocks containing the data usually do not match the logical numbers, so a translation is needed to locate each block. The file-organization module also includes the free-space manager, which tracks unallocated and provides these blocks to the file organization module when requested.

The logical file system uses the directory structure to provide the file-organization module with the information the latter needs, given a symbolic file name. The logical file system is also responsible for protection and security.

To create a new file, an application program calls the logical file system. The logical file system knows the format of the directory structures. To create a new file, it reads the appropriate directory into memory, updates it with the new entry, and writes it back to the disk.

Once the file is found the associated information such as size, owner, access permissions and data block locations are generally copied into a table in memory, referred to as the open-file fable, consisting of information about all the currently opened files.

The first reference to a file (normally an open) causes the directory structure to be searched and the directory entry for this file to be copied into the table of opened files. The index into this table is returned to the user program, and all further references are made through the index rather than with a symbolic name.

The name given to the index varies. Unix systems refer to it as a file descriptor, Windows/NT as a file handle, and other systems as a file control block.

Consequently, as long as the file is not closed, all file operations are done on the open-file table. When the file is closed by all users that have opened it, the updated file information is copied back to the disk-based directory structure.

File-System Mounting

- As a file must be opened before it is used, a file system must be mounted before it can be available to processes on the system. The mount procedure is straight forward. The stem is given the name of the device, and the location within the file structure at which to attach the file system (called the mount point).

- The operating system verifies that the device contains a valid file system. It does so by asking the device driver to read the device directory and verifying that the directory has the expected format. Finally, the operating system notes in its directory structure that a file system is mounted at the specified mount point. This scheme enables the operating system to traverse its directory structure, switching among file systems as appropriate.

Allocation Methods

- The direct-access nature of disks allows us flexibility in the implementation of files. Three major methods of allocating disk space are in wide use: contiguous, linked and indexed. Each method has its advantages and disadvantages.

Contiguous Allocation

- The contiguous allocation method requires each file to occupy a set of contiguous blocks on the disk. Disk addresses define a linear ordering on the disk. Notice that with this ordering assuming that only one job is accessing the disk, accessing block b + 1 after block b normally requires no head movement.

- When head movement is needed, it is only one track. Thus, the number of disk seeks required for accessing contiguously allocated files is minimal.

- Contiguous allocation of a file is defined by the disk address and length (in block units) of the first block. If the file is n blocks long, and starts at location!), then it occupies blocks b, b + 1, b + 2, ..., b + n − 1. The directory entry for each file indicates the address of the starting block and the length of the area allocate for this file.

- Accessing a file that has been allocated contiguously is easy. For sequential access, the file system remembers the disk address of the last block referenced and, when necessary, reads the next block. For direct access to block i of a file that starts at block b, we can immediately access block b + i. The contiguous disk-space-allocation problem can be seen to be a particular application of the general dynamic storage-allocation First Fit and Best Fit are the most common strategies used to select a free hole from the set of available holes. Simulations have shown that both first-fit and best-fit are more efficient than worst-fit in terms of both time and storage utilization. Neither first-fit nor best-fit is clearly best in terms of storage utilization, but first-fit is generally faster.

- These algorithms suffer from the problem of external fragmentation. As files are allocated and deleted, the free disk space is broken into little pieces. External fragmentation exists whenever free space is broken into chunks. It becomes a problem when the largest contiguous chunks is insufficient for a request; storage is fragmented into a number of holes, no one of which is large enough to store the data. Depending on the total amount of disk storage and the average file size, external fragmentation may be either a minor or a major problem.

- To prevent loss of significant amounts of disk space to external fragmentation, the user had to run repacking routine that copied the entire file system onto another floppy disk or onto a tape. The original floppy disk was then freed completely, creating one large contiguous free space. The routine then copied the files back onto the floppy disk by allocating contiguous space from this one large hole. This scheme effectively compacts all free space into one contiguous space, solving the fragmentation problem. The cost of this compaction is time.

- The time cost is particularly severe for large hard disks that use contiguous allocation, where compacting all the space may take hours and may be necessary on a weekly basis. During this down time, normal system operation generally cannot be permitted, so such compaction is avoided at all costs on production machines.

- A major problem is determining how much space is needed for a file. When the file is created, the total amount of space it will need must be found and allocated.

- The user will normally over estimate the amount of space needed, resulting in considerable wasted space.

Linked Allocation

- Linked allocation solves all problems of contiguous allocation. With link allocation, each file is a linked list disk blocks; the disk blocks may be scattered anywhere on the disk.
- This pointer is initialized to nil (the end-of-list pointer value) to signify an empty file. The size field is also set to 0. A write to the file causes a free bio to be found via the free-space management system, and this new block is the written to, and is linked to the end of the file
- There is no external fragmentation with linked allocation, and any free! block on the free-space list can be used to satisfy a request. Notice also that there is no need to declare the size of a file when that file is created. A file can continue to grow as long as there are free blocks. Consequently, it is never necessary to compact disk space.
- The major problem is that it can be used effectively for only sequential access files. To find the ith block of a file we must start at the beginning of that file, and follow the pointers until we get to the ith block. Each access to a pointer requires a disk read and sometimes a disk seek. Consequently, it is inefficient to support a direct-access capability for linked allocation files.
- Linked allocation is the space required for the pointers If a pointer requires 4 bytes out of a 512 Byte block then 0.78 percent of the disk is being used for pointer, rather than for information.
- The usual solution to this problem is to collect blocks into multiples, called clusters, and to allocate the clusters rather than blocks. For instance, the file system define a cluster as 4 blocks and operate on the disk in only cluster units.
- Pointers then use a much smaller percentage of the file's disk space. This method allows the logical-to-physical block mapping to remain simple, but

improves disk throughput (fewer disk head seeks) and decreases the space needed for block allocation and free-list management. The cost of this approach an increase in internal fragmentation.

- Yet another problem is reliability. Since the files are linked together by pointers scattered all over the disk, consider what would happen if a pointer— were lost or damaged. Partial solutions are to use doubly linked lists or to store the file name and relative block number in each block; however, these schemes require even more overhead for each file.

- An important variation, on the linked allocation method is the use of a file allocation table (FAT). This simple but efficient method of disk-space allocation is used by the MS-DOS and OS/2 operating systems. A section of disk at the beginning of each-partition is set aside to contain the table. The table has one entry for each disk block, and is indexed by block number. The FAT is used much as is a linked list. The directory entry contains the block number of the first block of the file. The table entry indexed by that block number then contains the block number of the next block in the file. This chain continues until the last block, which has a special end-of-file value -as the table entry. Unused blocks are indicated by a 0 table value. Allocating a new block to a file is a simple matter of finding the first 0-valued table entry, and replacing the previous end-of-file value with the address of the new block. The 0 is then replaced with the end-offile value. An illustrative example is the FAT structure of for a file consisting of disk blocks 217, 618, and 339.

Indexed Allocation

- Linked allocation solves the external-fragmentation and size-declaration problems of contiguous allocation. The absence of a FAT, linked allocation cannot support efficient direct access, since the pointers to the blocks are scattered with the blocks themselves all over the disk and need to be retrieved in order Indexed allocation solves this problem by bringing all the pointers together into one location: the index block.
- Each file has its own index block, which is an array of disk-block addresses. The ith entry in the index block points to the ith block of the file. The directory contains the address of the index block.
- When the file is created, all pointers in the index block are set to nil. When the ith block is first written, a block is obtained: from the free space manager, and its address- is put in the ith index-block entry.
- Allocation supports direct access, without suffering from external fragmentation because any free block on he disk may satisfy a request for more space.
- Indexed allocation does suffer from wasted space. The pointer overhead of the index block is generally greater than the pointer overhead of linked allocation.
    1. **Linked scheme.** An index block is normally one disk block. Thus, it can be read and written directly by itself.
    2. **Multilevel index.** A variant of the linked representation is to use a first-level index block to point to a set of second-level index blocks, which in turn point to the file blocks. To access a block, the operating system uses the first-level index to find a second-level index block, and that block to find the desired data block.

Free-Space Management

Since there is only a limited amount of disk space, it is necessary to reuse the space from deleted files for new files, if possible.

Bit Vector

- Free-space list is implemented as a bit map or bit vector. Each block is represented by 1 bit. If the block is free, the bit is 1; if the block is allocated, the bit is 0.

- For example consider a disk where blocks 2, 3, 4, 5, 8, 9, 10, 11, 12, 13, 17, 18, 25, 26, and 27 are free, and the rest of the blocks are allocated. The free-space bit map would be

    00111100111111000110000011100000 .....

- The main advantage of this approach is that it is relatively simple and efficient to find the first free block or n consecutive free blocks on the disk.

- The calculation of the block number is

(number of bits per word) x (number of 0-value words) + offset of first 1 bit

Linked List

- Another approach is to link together all the free disk blocks, keeping a pointy to the first free block in a special location on the disk and caching it in memory. This first block contains a pointer to the next free disk block, and so on. Block 2 would contain a pointer to block 3, which would point to block 4, which would point to block 5, which would point to block 8, and so on. Usually, the operating system simply needs a free block so that it can allocate that block to a file, so the first block in the free list is used.

Grouping

- A modification of the free-list approach is to store the addresses of n free blocks in the first free block. The first n-1 of these blocks are actually free. The importance of this implementation is that the addresses of a large number of free blocks can be found quickly, unlike in the standard linked-list approach.

Counting

- Several contiguous blocks may be allocated or freed simultaneously, particularly when space is allocated with the contiguous allocation algorithm or through clustering. A list of n free disk addresses, we can keep the address of the first free block and the number n of free contiguous blocks that follow the first block.
- Each entry in the free-space list then consists of a disk address and a count. Although each entry requires more space than would a simple disk address, the overall list will be shorter, as long as count is generally greater than 1.

14.9 Summary

A file is an abstract data type defined and implemented by the operating system. It is a sequence of logical records. A logical record may be a byte, a line, or a more complex data item. The operating system may specifically support various record types or may leave that support to the application program.

The major task for the operating system is to map the logical file concept onto physical storage devices such as magnetic tape or disk. All the file information kept in the directory structure. File system is implemented on the disk and memory.

Disk address define a linear addressing on the disk. Continuous allocation algorithm suffers from the external fragmentation. Free space management techniques are bit vector, linked list. Grouping, counting.

Since file are the main information storage mechanism in most computer systems, file protection is needed. Access to files can be controlled separately for each type of access – read, write, execute, append, delete, list directory, and so on. File protection can be provided by access lists, passwords, or other techniques.

14.10 Model Question

Q.1 Explain the file concept?
Q.2 List the different types of files?
Q.3 Describe the different types of access methods?
Q.4 What are the advantages and disadvantages of continuous, linked and indexed allocation methods?
Q.5 Explain the file system structure?
Q.6 What are different types of partitions and mounting?

CHAPTER 13
PROTECTION

Unit Structure
13.0 Objectives

13.1 Goals of Protection

13.2 Domain of Protection

13.3 Access Matrix

13.4 Revocation of Access Rights

13.5 Summary

13.6 Model Question

13.0 Objective
- Discuss the goals and principles of protection in a modern computer system.
- Explain how protection domains combined with an access matrix are used to specify the resources a process may access.
- Examine capability and language-based protection systems

13.1 Goals of Protection
Protection can improve reliability by detecting latent errors at the interfaces between component subsystems. Early detection of interface errors can often prevent contamination of a healthy subsystem by a malfunctioning subsystem. Also, an unprotected resource cannot defend against use by an unauthorized or incompetent user. A protection oriented system provides means to distinguish between authorized and unauthorized usage.

The role of protection in a computer system is to provide a mechanism for the enforcement of the policies governing resource use. These policies can be established in a variety of ways. Some are fixed in the design of the system, while others are formulated by the management of a system. Still others are defined by the individual users to protect their own files and programs. A protection system must have the flexibility to enforce a variety of policies. The application programmer needs to use protection mechanism.

13.2 Principles of Protection
- Frequently, a guiding principle can be used throughout a project, such as the design of an operating system. Following this principle simplifies design decisions and keeps the system consistent and easy to understand. A key, time tested guiding principle for protection is the principle of least privilege. It dictates that programs, users, and even systems be given just enough privileges to perform their tasks.

- An operating system following the principle of least privilege implements its features, programs, system calls, and data structures so that failure or compromise of a component does the minimum damage and allows the minimum damage to be done.

- The principle of least privilege can help produce a more secure computing environment.

13.3 Domain of Protection

- A computer system is a collection of processes and objects. By objects, we mean both hardware objects (such as the CPU, memory segments, printers, disks, tape drives), and software objects (such as files, programs, and semaphore).

- Protection domain is process that operates within a protection domain, which specifies the resources that the process may access. Each domain defines a set of objects and .the types of operations that may be invoked on each object.

- The ability to execute an operation on an object is an access right. A domain is a collection of access ' rights, each of which is an ordered pair <object-name, rights-set>. For example, if domain D has the access right <file F, {read, write}>, then a process executing in domain D can both read and write file F, if cannot, however, perform any other operation on that object.

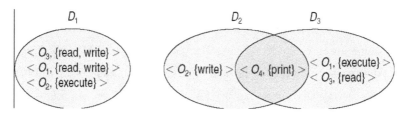

Fig System with three protection domains.

- Domains do not need to be disjoint; they may share access rights. The association between a process and a domain may be either static or dynamic. A domain can be realized in a variety of ways:

1. Each user may be a domain. The set of objects that can be accessed depends on the identity of the user. Domain switching occur when the user is changed — generally when one user logs out and another user logs in.
2. Each process may be a domain. In this case, the set of objects that can be accessed depends on the identity of the process. Domain switching corresponds to one process sending a message to another process, and then waiting for a response.
3. Each procedure may be a domain. In this case, the set of objects that can be accessed corresponds to the local variables define Domain switching occurs when a procedure call is made.

13.3 Access Matrix

- Our model of protection can be viewed abstractly as a matrix, called an access matrix. The rows of the access matrix represent domains, and the columns represent objects. Each entry in the matrix consists of a set of access rights.

- Because objects are defined explicitly by the column, we can omit the object name from the access right. The entry access (i, j) defines the set of operations that a process, executing in domain D_i, can invoke on object O_j.

- We consider the access matrix shown in Figure. There are four domains and four objects: three files (F1, F2, F3), and one laser printer. When a process executes in domain D1, it can read files F1 and F3.. A process executing in domain D4 has the same privileges as it does in domain D1, but in addition, it can also write onto files F1 and F3. Note that the laser printer can be accessed only by a process executing in domain D2.

- The access-matrix scheme provides us with the mechanism for specifying a variety of policies. More specifically, we must ensure that a process executing in domain Di can access only those objects specified in row i, and then only as allowed by the access matrix entries.

Object Domain	F1	F2	F3	printer
D1	Read		Read	
D2				Print
D3		read	Execute	
D4	Read write		Read write	

Fig Access Matrix

- Policy decisions concerning protection can be implemented by the access matrix. The users normally decide the contents of the access-matrix entries.
- Allowing controlled change to the contents of the access-matrix entries requires three additional operations: **copy, owner, and control.**

13.4 Revocation of Access Rights

In a dynamic protection system, we may sometimes need to revolve access rights to objects shared by different users. Various questions about revocation may arise:

- **Immediate versus delayed.** Does revocation occur immediately, or is it delayed? If revocation is delayed, can we find out when it will take place?

- **Selective versus general.** When an access right to an object revoked, does it affect all the users who have an access right to that object, or can we specify a select group of users whose access rights should be revoked?
- **Partial versus total.** Can a subset of the rights associated with an object be revoked, or must we revoke all access rights for this object?
- **Temporary versus permanent.** Can access be revoked permanently (that is, the revoked access right will never again be available), or can access be revoked and later be obtained again?

Schemes that implements revocation for capabilities include the following:
- **Reacquisition.** Periodically, capabilities are deleted from each domain. If a process wants to use a capability, it may find that capability has been deleted. The process may then try to reacquire the capability. If access has been revoked, the process will not be able to reacquire the capability.
- **Back pointers.** A list of pointers is maintained with each object, pointing to all capabilities associated with that object. When revocation is required, we can follow this pointers, changing the capabilities as necessary. This scheme was adopted in the MULTICS system.
- **Indirection.** The capabilities point indirectly, not directly, to the objects. Each capability points to a unique entry in a global trade, which in turn points to the object. We implement revocation by searching the global table for the desired entry and deleting it. It does not allow selective revocation.
- **Keys.** A key is a unique bit pattern that can be associated with a capability. This key is defined when the capability is created, and it can be neither modifier\ed nor inspected by the process that owns the capability. A master

key is associated with each object; it can be defined or replaced with the set-key operation.

13.5 Summary

Computer system contains many objects, and they need to be protected from misuse. Objects may be hardware (such as memory, CPU time, and I/O devices) or software(such as files, programs, and semaphores). An access right is permission to perform an operation on an object. A domain is a set of access rights. Processes execute in domains and may use any of the access rights in the domain to access and manipulate objects. During its lifetime, a process may be either bound to a protection domain or allowed to switch from one domain to another.

The access matrix is a general model of protection that provides a mechanism for protection without imposing a particular protection policy on the system or its users. The separation of policy and mechanism is an important design policy.

Real systems are much more limited than the general model and tend to provide protection for files.

13.6 Model Question

Q. 1 Define and explain Access matrix?
Q. 2 How does the systems that implement the principle of least privilege still have protection systems?
Q.3 Discuss strengths and weaknesses of implementing an access matrix using access list?
Q. 4 Explain Domain Structure?

CHAPTER 14
SECURITY

Unit Structure

14.0 Objective

- To discuss security threats and attacks.
- To explain the fundamentals of encryption, authentication, and hashing.
- To examine the uses of cryptography in computing.
- To describe the various countermeasures to security attacks.

14.1 The Security Problem

The operating system can allow users to protect their resources. We say that a system is secure if its resources art used and accessed as intended under all circumstances. Unfortunately, it is not generally possible to achieve total security. Security violations of the system can be categorized as being either intentional (malicious) or accidental. Among the forms of malicious access are the following:

• Unauthorized reading of data (theft of information).

• Unauthorized modification of data.

• Unauthorized destruction of data.

To protect the system, we must take security measures at two levels:

• **Physical:** The site or sites containing the computer systems must be physically secured against armed or surreptitious entry by intruders.

• **Human:** Users must be screened carefully so that the chance of authorizing a user who then gives access to an intruder (in exchange for a bribe, for example) is reduced.

Security at both levels must be maintained if operating-system security is to be ensured.

Fig 14.1 Standard Security Attack.

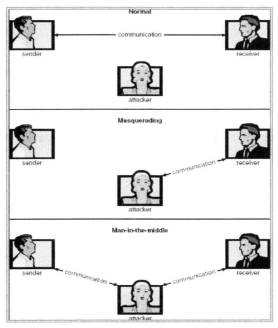

14.2 Authentication

A major security problem for operating systems is the authentication problem. The protection system depends on an ability to identify the programs and processes that are executing. Authentication is based on one or more of three items: user possession (a key or card), user knowledge (a user identifier and password), and a user attribute (fingerprint) retina pattern, or signature).

❖ Constraining set of potential senders of a message

  ➢ Complementary and sometimes redundant to encryption.

  ➢ Also can prove message unmodified.

❖ An authentication algorithm consists of following components:

  ➢ A set K of keys.

  ➢ A set M of messages.

  ➢ A set A of authenticators.

  ➢ A function $S : K \rightarrow (M \rightarrow A)$

    ▪ That is, for each $k \in K$, $S(k)$ is a function for generating authenticators from messages.

    ▪ Both S and $S(k)$ for any k should be efficiently computable functions.

  ➢ A function $V : K \rightarrow (M \times A \rightarrow \{true, false\})$. That is, for each $k \in K$, $V(k)$ is a function for verifying authenticators on messages.

    ▪ Both V and $V(k)$ for any k should be efficiently computable functions.

❖ For a message m, a computer can generate an authenticator $a \in A$ such that $V(k)(m, a) = true$ only if it possesses $S(k)$.

❖ Thus, computer holding $S(k)$ can generate authenticators on messages so that any other computer possessing $V(k)$ can verify them.

❖ Computer not holding $S(k)$ cannot generate authenticators on messages that can be verified using $V(k)$.

❖ Since authenticators are generally exposed (for example, they are sent on the network with the messages themselves), it must not be feasible to derive $S(k)$ from the authenticators.

Authentication – Hash Functions
  ➢ Basis of authentication.
  ➢ Creates small, fixed-size block of data (**message digest, hash value**) from m.
  ➢ Hash Function H must be collision resistant on m
     • Must be infeasible to find an $m' \neq m$ such that $H(m) = H(m')$.
  ➢ If $H(m) = H(m')$, then $m = m'$
     • The message has not been modified.
  ➢ Common message-digest functions include **MD5**, which produces a 128-bit hash, and **SHA-1**, which outputs a 160-bit hash.

Authentication – MAC
❖ Symmetric encryption used in **message-authentication code (MAC)** authentication algorithm.

❖ Simple example:

  ➢ MAC defines $S(k)(m) = f(k, H(m))$.

     ▪ Where f is a function that is one-way on its first argument.

        • k cannot be derived from $f(k, H(m))$.

     ▪ Because of the collision resistance in the hash function, reasonably assured no other message could create the same MAC.

     ▪ A suitable verification algorithm is $V(k)(m, a) \equiv (f(k,m) = a)$.

     ▪ Note that k is needed to compute both $S(k)$ and $V(k)$, so anyone able to compute one can compute the other.

Authentication – Digital Signature

❖ Based on asymmetric keys and digital signature algorithm.

❖ Authenticators produced are **digital signatures.**

❖ In a digital-signature algorithm, computationally infeasible to derive $S(k_s)$ from $V(k_v)$

  ➤ V is a one-way function.

  ➤ Thus, k_v is the public key and k_s is the private key.

❖ Consider the RSA digital-signature algorithm.

  ➤ Similar to the RSA encryption algorithm, but the key use is reversed

  ➤ Digital signature of message $S(k_s)(m) = H(m)^{ks} \bmod N$

  ➤ The key k_s again is a pair d, N, where N is the product of two large, randomly chosen prime numbers p and q.

  ➤ Verification algorithm is $V(k_v)(m, a) \equiv (a^{kv} \bmod N = H(m))$

    ▪ Where k_v satisfies $k_v k_s \bmod (p - 1)(q - 1) = 1$

❖ Why authentication if a subset of encryption?

  ➤ Fewer computations (except for RSA digital signatures).

  ➤ Authenticator usually shorter than message.

  ➤ It Can be basis for **non-repudiation.**

14.3 One Time passwords

• To avoid the problems of password sniffing and shoulder surfing, a system could use a set of paired passwords. When a session begins, the system randomly selects and presents one part of a password pair; the user must supply the other part. In this system, the user is challenged and must respond with the correct answer to that challenge.

- This approach can be generalized to the use of an algorithm as a password. The algorithm might be an integer function.
- In this one-time password system, the password is different in each instance. Anyone capturing the password from one session and trying to reuse it in another session will fail.
- The user uses the keypad to enter the shared secret, also known as a personal identification number (PIN). Another variation on one-time passwords is the use of a code book, or one time pad.

14.4 Program Threats

In an environment where a program written by one user may be used by another user, there is an opportunity for misuse, which may result in unexpected behavior. There are two common methods. Trojan horses and Trap doors.

14.4.1 Trojan Horse

- Many systems have mechanisms for allowing programs written by users to be executed by other users. If these programs are executed in a domain that provides the access rights of the executing user, they may misuse these rights.
- A code segment that its environment is called a Trojan horse. The Trojan-horse problem is exacerbated by long search paths. The search path lists the set of directories to search when an ambiguous program name is given. The path is searched for a file of that name and the file is executed. All the directories in the search path must be secure, or a Trojan horse could be slipped into the user's path and executed accidentally.

- A variation of the Trojan horse would be a program that emulates a login program. The emulator stored away the password, printed out a login error message, and exited; the user was then provided with a genuine login prompt.
- This type of attack can be defeated by the operating system printing a usage message at the end of an interactive session or by a non-trappable key sequence, such as the control-alt-delete combination that Windows NT uses.

14.4.2 Trap Door

The designer of a program or system might leave a hole in the software that only Operating System is capable of using. A clever trap door could be included in a compiler. The compiler could generate standard object code as well as a trap door, regardless of the source code being compiled.

14.5 System Threats

Most operating systems provide a means for processes to spawn other processes.

14.5.1 Worms

- A worm is a process that uses the spawn mechanism to clobber system performance. The worm spawns copies of itself, using up system resources and perhaps locking out system use by, all other processes. Since they may reproduce themselves among systems and thus shut down the entire network.
- The worm was made up of two programs a grappling hook (also called bootstrap or vector) program and the main program. The grappling hook consisted of 99 lines of C code compiled and run on each machine it accessed. The grappling hook connected to the machine where it originated

and uploaded a copy of the main worm onto the "hooked" system. The main program proceeded to search for other machines to which the newly infected system could connect easily.

- The attack via remote access was one of three infection methods built into the worm.

14.5.2 Viruses

- Another form of computer attack is a virus. Like worms, viruses are designed to spread into other programs and can wreak havoc in a system, including modifying or destroying files and causing system crashes and program malfunctions. Whereas a worm is structured as a complete, standalone program, a virus is a fragment of code embedded in a legitimate program. Viruses are a major problem for computer users, especially users of microcomputer systems.

- Even if a virus does infect a program, its powers are limited because other aspects of the system are protected in multi-user. Single-user systems have no such protections and, as a result, a virus has free run.

- Viruses are usually spread by users downloading viral programs from public bulletin boards or exchanging floppy disks containing an infection. The best protection against computer viruses is prevention, or the practice of Safe computing.

14.6 Threat Monitoring

- The security of a system can be improved by two management techniques. One is threat monitoring: The system can check for suspicious patterns of activity in an attempt to detect a security violation.
- Another technique is an audit log. An audit log simply records the time, user, and type of all accesses to an object. Networked computers are much more susceptible to security attacks than are standalone systems.
- One solution is the use of a firewall to separate trusted and un-trusted systems. A firewall is a computer or router that sits between the trusted and the un-trusted. It limits network access between the two security domains, and monitors and logs all connections. A firewall therefore may need to allow http to pass.

14.7 Encryption

- Encryption is one common method of protecting information transmitted over unreliable links. The basic mechanism works as follows.
    1. The information (text) is encrypted (encoded) from its initial readable form (called clear text), to an internal form (called cipher text). This internal text form, although readable, does not make any sense.
    2. The cipher text can be stored in a readable file, or transmitted over unprotected channels.
    3. To make sense of the cipher text, the receiver must decrypt (decode) it back into clear text.

Even if the encrypted information is accessed by an unauthorized person or program, it will be useless unless it can be decoded.

❖ Encryption algorithm consists of

➢ Set of K keys.

- ➤ Set of M Messages.

- ➤ Set of C ciphertexts (encrypted messages).

- ➤ A function $E : K \rightarrow (M \rightarrow C)$. That is, for each $k \in K$, $E(k)$ is a function for generating ciphertexts from messages.

  - ▪ Both E and $E(k)$ for any k should be efficiently computable functions.

- ➤ A function $D : K \rightarrow (C \rightarrow M)$. That is, for each $k \in K$, $D(k)$ is a function for generating messages from ciphertexts.

  - ▪ Both D and $D(k)$ for any k should be efficiently computable functions.

- ❖ An encryption algorithm must provide this essential property: Given a ciphertext $c \in C$, a computer can compute m such that $E(k)(m) = c$ only if it possesses $D(k)$.

- ➤ Thus, a computer holding $D(k)$ can decrypt ciphertexts to the plaintexts used to produce them, but a computer not holding $D(k)$ cannot decrypt ciphertexts.

- ❖ Since ciphertexts are generally exposed (for example, sent on the network), it is important that it be infeasible to derive $D(k)$ from the ciphertexts.

14.8 Computer Security Classifications

- • The U.S. Department of Defense outlines four divisions of computer security: **A**, **B**, **C**, and **D**.
- • **D** – Minimal security.
- • **C** – Provides discretionary protection through auditing. Divided into **C1** and **C2**. **C1** identifies cooperating users with the same level of protection. **C2** allows user-level access control.
- • **B** – All the properties of **C**, however each object may have unique sensitivity labels. Divided into **B1**, **B2**, and **B3**.
- • **A** – Uses formal design and verification techniques to ensure security.

14.9 Summary

Protection is an internal problem. Security, in contrast, must consider both the computer system and the environment people, buildings, businesses, valuable objects, and threats within which the system is used.

The data stored in the computer system must be protected from unauthorized access, malicious destruction or alteration, and accidental introduction of inconsistency. It is easier to protect against accidental loss of data consistency than to protect against malicious access to the data.

Several types of attacks can be launched against programs and against individual computes or the masses. Encryption limits the domain of receivers of data, while authentication limits the domain of senders. User authentication methods are used to identify legitimate users of a system.

14.10 Model Question

Q. 1 Define and explain Encryption?

Q. 2 Explain authentication process?

Q. 3 Explain various types of system threats?

Q.4 Write a note on following
    a)   viruses
    b)   Computer Security Specification

Q. 5 Explain types of Program threats?

CHAPTER 15
LINUX SYSTEM

Unit Structure

15.0 Objectives

15.1 Linux introduction and File System

15.2 Basic Features

15.3 Advantages

15.4 Basic Architecture of UNIX/Linux System

15.5 Summary

15.6 Model Question

15.0 Objective

- To explore the history of the UNIX operating system from which Linux is derived and the principles which Linux is designed upon.

- To examine the Linux process model and illustrate how Linux schedules processes and provides inter-process communication.

- To explore how Linux implements file systems and manages I/O devices.

15.1 Linux introduction and File System

Linux looks like UNIX system. Linux is developed by Linux Torvalds. Linux development began in 1991. Linux source code is available for free on the internet. The basic Linux system is standard environment for applications and user programming.

15.1.1 Components of a Linux System
Any Linux system consists of three components.
1. Kernel
2. System libraries
3. System utilities

Kernel:
The Kernel is responsible for maintaining all the important abstraction of the operating system. It includes virtual memory and processes. Kernel is most important component of the Linux system.

System libraries:

It contains standard set of functions through which application can interact with the Kernel. System library implements much of the operating system functionality that does not need the full privileges of Kernel code.

System utilities:
System utilities are programs that perform individual, specialized management tasks.

- Fig.15.1 shows the components of the Linux system.
- All the Kernel code executes in the processors privileged mode with full access to all the physical resources of the computer. Linux refers to this privileged mode as Kernel mode. In Linux, no user mode code is built into the Kernel.

System Management programs	User Processes	User utility programs	Compilers
System shared libraries			
Linux Kernel			
Loadable Kernel modules			

Fig. 15.1 Components of Linux system

- Any operating system support code that does not need to urn in Kernel mode is placed into the system libraries instead.
- The Kernel is created as a single, monolithic binary. All Kernel code and data structures are kept in a single address space, no context switches are necessary when a process calls an operating system function. Core scheduling, virtual memory code also occupied same address space.
- Linux Kernel provides all the functionality necessary to run processes, and it provides system services to give arbitrated and protected access to hardware resources
- The Linux system includes a wide variety of user mode programs both system utilities and user utilities.

15.2 Kernel Modules
- Kernel code executes in Kernel mode with full access to all the physical resources of the computer. Sections of Kernel code that can be compiled, loaded and unloaded independent of the rest of the Kernel.

- A Kernel module may typically implement a device driver, a file system, or a networking protocol. The module interface allows third parties to write and distribute, on their own teams, device drivers or file systems that could not be distributed under the GPL.
- The loadable Kernel modules run in privileged Kernel mode. Kernel modules allow a Linux system to be setup with a standard, minimal Kernel, without any extra device drivers built in. Kernel management allows modules to be dynamically loaded into memory when needed.
- Linux Kernel modules has three component.
    1. Module management
    2. Driver registration
    3. Conflict resolution mechanism

1. Module management
1. It support loading modules into memory and letting them talk to the rest of the Kernel.
2. Linux maintains an internal symbol table in the Kernel.
3. Module loading is split into two separate sections:
a. Managing sections of module code in Kernel memory
b. Handling symbols that modules are allowed to reference.
4. Symbol table does not contain the full set of symbol defined in the Kernel during latter compilation
5. The module requestor manages loading requested, but currently unloaded modules.
6. It also regularly queries the Kernel to see whether a dynamically loaded module is still in use and will unload it when it is no longer actively needed
7. Original service request will complete once the module is loaded.

2. Driver Registration.
1. Allows modules to tell the rest of the kernel that a new driver has become available.
2. Kernel maintains dynamic tables of all known drivers.
3. Kernel also provides a set of routines to allow drivers to be added or removed.
4. Registration table contains following:
        a. Device drivers
        b. File systems
        c. Network protocols
        d. Binary format.

5. Device drivers may be block or character devices.
6. Files system contains network file system, virtual file system etc.
7. Network protocol includes IPX, packet filtering rules for a network.

3. Conflict Resolution
1. A mechanisms that allows different device drivers to reserve hardware resources and to protect those resources from accidental use by another driver.
2. Linux provides a ventral conflict resolution mechanism.
3. Conflict resolution module aims are
    a. To prevent modules from clashing over access to hardware resources.
    b. Prevent auto probes from interfering with existing device drivers.
    c. Resolve conflicts among multiple drivers trying to access the same hardware.
4. Kernel maintains lists of allocated hardware resources.

15.3 Basic Features

UNIX has a number of features, mostly good and some bad, but it is necessary to know at least some of them:

1. UNIX is Portable: Portability is the ability of the software that operates on one machine to operate on another, different machine. In UNIX there are two types of portability, that of the UNIX operating system itself (i.e. the Kernel program) and of the application program.

Advantages of portability are:
a) Portable application program decrease the programming costs.
b) Retraining is avoided as the end user works on a similar system with enhanced capabilities.

2. Open system: The system that more than one system can access the same data at the same time. Several people involved in a common project can conveniently access each other's data. Apart from data, other resources like memory (RAM), the CPU(the chip), or the hard disk can be used by many users simultaneously.

3. Multi-user Capability: This means that more than one system can access the same data at the same time. Several people involved in a common project can conveniently access each other's data. Apart from data, other resources like memory(RAM), the CPU(the chip), or the hard disk can be used by many users simultaneously.

4. Multi-tasking Capability: Multi-tasking means that a user can perform more than one tasks at the same time. A user can do this by placing some tasks in the background while he works on a task in the foreground. An ampersand(&) placed at the end of the command line sends the process in background.

5. Hierarchical File System: Hierarchical structure offers maximum flexibility for grouping information in a way that reflects in natural structure. The programs and data can be organized conveniently since files can be grouped according to usage.

6. The shell: User interaction with UNIX is controlled by the shell, a powerful command interpreter. The shell has various capabilities like redirecting the application input and output and also to progress a group of files with a single command.

7. UNIX has built in networking: The UNIX has various built in programs and utilities like UUCP, mail, write, etc. With these utilities one can communicate with other user or one server to another.

8. Security: Computer system security means protecting hardware and the information contained within the system. Security means to avoid:

a) Unauthorized access to the computer system.

b) Unauthorized examination of output.

c) Unauthorized tapping of data.

d) Destruction of software data by mistake or on purpose.

e) Examination of sensitive data by unauthorized users and alteration of sensitive data without detection.

The UNIX provides the features like:

a) Password protection for system access.

b) Control access to individual files.

c) Encryption of data files.

9. Software Development Tools: UNIX offers an excellent variety of tools for software development for all phases, from program editing to maintenance of software.

15.4 Basic Architecture of UNIX/Linux System

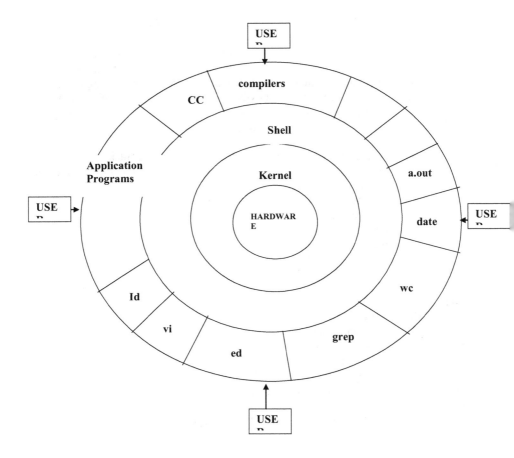

Fig Architecture of UNIX System

The figure shows the architecture of the UNIX system in the form of various layers. The inner most layer i.e. core is the hardware of the computer system. The kernel is a software which directly comes in contact with the hardware and controls the hardware. A layer above this is the shell. Above this the various utilities like nroff, troff, vi, as, etc. and the various compilers and other application program reside. Let us see these layers and their functions in detail:

1. Hardware: The hardware at the centre of the structure provides the operating system with basic services. The hardware constitutes all the peripherals like memory (RAM, HDD, FDD, CD etc), processor, mouse and other input devices, terminal (i.e. VDUs), printers etc.

2. The Kernel: The operating system interacts directly with the hardware, providing common services to programs and insulating user program complexities of hardware. The operating system is also called as Kernel. This kernel interacts directly with the hardware. Because of this hardware isolation of user program, it is easy to move the user programs easily between UNIX systems running on different hardware.

3. Shell: Shell is actually the interface between the user and the Kernel that isolates the user from knowledge of Kernel functions. The shell accepts the commands keyed in by the users and checks for their syntax and gives out error messages if something goes. These command after getting interpreted by the shell are provided to kernel for appropriate action. It also provides the features of pipe (|) and redirection (i.e. <, >, >>, <<). The shell also has a programming capability of its own. There are a number of shells available in various UNIX flavours but common are-

a) Bourne Shell (sh)

b) C Shell (csh)

c) Korn Shell (ksh)

The other shells are: bash, restricted Shell(rsh) and visual Shell(vsh). The bourne Shell (sh) is also called a standard shell.

4. UNIX utilities: The UNIX system Kernel does only level jobs necessary to schedule processes, keep track of files, and control hardware devices.

All other operating system functions are done by utility programs written as software tools.

Following are some of the utilities that play a prominent role in the operating of the UNIX system.

a) **Init** initializes the process creation mechanism.

For each terminal where a login is allowed, init creates a process that prints the login: message.

b) **Getty** process "conditions" the connection to the terminal so that the terminal can communicate with the computer and then prints the login: message.

c) **Login** when an user responds to the login prompt the login program replaces getty. If the user account has a password, login prints the password : message and checks to see that the password entered is correct.

If correct, program named in password file, usually Bourne shell or C shell replaces login and the user is successfully logged into the system.

d) **stty** changes a terminal characteristics.

e) **mkfs** builds a file system.

f) **mknod** builds a special file system.

g) **mount unmount** mounts and unmounts a file system.

h) **syne** writes a disk block images from memory to disk.

15.5 Summary

Linux is a modern, free operating system based on UNIX standards. It has designed to run efficiently and reliably on common PC hardware; it also runs on a variety of other platforms. It provide a programming interface and user interface compatible with standard UNIX systems and can run a large number of UNIX applications, including an increasing number of commercially supported applications.

Linux has not evolved in a vacuum a completely Linux system includes many components that were developed independently of Linux. The core Linux operating system kernel is entirely original, but allows much existing free UNIX software to run, resulting in a entire UNIX compatible operating system free from proprietary code.

The Linux kernel is implemented as a traditional monolithic kernel for performance reasons, but it is modular enough in design to allow most drivers to be dynamically loaded and unloaded at run time.

15.6 Model Question

Q.1 List different components of a linux system?

Q.2 What are Kernel modules?

Q.3 Explain Basic architecture of UNIX/Linux system?

Q.4 Explain basic features of UNIX/Linux?

Q.5 Define and explain Shell?

www.ingramcontent.com/pod-product-compliance
Lightning Source LLC
Chambersburg PA
CBHW071201050326
40689CB00011B/2210